FOOTPRINTS ON CONCRETE

The Story of a Barefoot
Dreamer Who Refused to Quit

ADEOLA AJAYI

Copyright © 2025 by Adeola Ajayi

JM Publishing LLC

All rights reserved. No part of this publication may be reproduced, stored or transmitted in any form or by any means, electronic, mechanical, photocopying, recording, scanning, or otherwise without written permission from the publisher. It is illegal to copy this book, post it to a website, or distribute it by any other means without permission.

Adeola Ajayi asserts the moral right to be identified as the author of this work.

Adeola Ajayi has no responsibility for the persistence or accuracy of URLs for external or third-party internet websites referred to in this publication and does not guarantee that any content on such websites is, or will remain, accurate or appropriate.

Designations used by companies to distinguish their products are often claimed as trademarks. All brand names and product names used in this book and on its cover are trade names, service marks, trademarks, and registered trademarks of their respective owners. The publishers and the book are not associated with any product or vendor mentioned in this book. None of the companies referenced within the book have endorsed the book.

First Edition

ISBN: 979-8-9925359-5-2 (Paperback)
      979-8-9925359-4-5 (Hardcover)

To the dreamers walking barefoot through hard places:
This is for you.

For the ones who were told they were too small, too poor, too broken to rise:
You were always enough.

And to my late father, Idowu "ID Noble" Ajayi:
Your legacy lives on through every step I take.

The ground beneath your feet may be cracked and cruel,
but keep walking.
Each step leaves a mark.
Each footprint is proof you survived.

—Adeola Ajayi

CONTENTS

Foreword. i

Preface. iii

Acknowledgments v

Prologue xi

Welcome. xv

Part One   1

1. Where It All Began 3

2. Growing Up in Lagos 9

3. The Classroom 15

4. Barefoot Dreams 21

5. The Day My Brother Dragged Me to School III. 31

6. A New Kind of Court. 39

7. Coach Peter's House .45

Part Two 53

8. The American Dream Begins 55

9. Proving Myself 63

10. The Fall 69

11. The Door That Didn't Close .75

12. Dr. Jackie and a New Home .81

Part Three 87

13. The Setback No One Saw 89

14. Surgery and Survival 95

15. From Pain to Purpose: The AOA Foundation 103

16. Where My Feet Now Stand 109

17. Bonus Chapter: A Letter to My Father, ID Noble 115

18. Bonus Chapter: Dr. Jackie, My Mother, My Miracle 119

19. Bonus Chapter: Coach Curtis Berry, My Father, My Foundation . . 123

20. Bonus Chapter: A Letter to My Younger Self 127

21. Bonus Chapter: What the Concrete Taught Me 131

22. Images 135

Appendix: The AOA Foundation's Impact 159

Call to Action 163

About the Author 165

Foreword

by Dr. Jackie Walters,
physician, mother, believer in miracles

Some stories are told to entertain. Others, to inform.

But every now and then, a story arrives like a knock on your heart—not to pass the time but to change the direction of your life.

Footprints on Concrete is one of those stories.

This book is not just pages and ink. It is a living, breathing testament to what happens when a child refuses to let his circumstances define him. I know this story intimately, not because I heard it but because I've watched it unfold.

I am the mother of the man who wrote this book.

And before the world knew his name, I knew his fight.

Adeola Ajayi was born not with a silver spoon but a soul-deep hunger, one that could not be satisfied by food alone. The kind of hunger that reached for something higher: for purpose, for meaning, for more.

He grew up in conditions most people will never fully fathom: barefoot on broken concrete, with a dream in his heart and no road map in his hand. But what he lacked in comfort, he made up for in conviction. And I've seen that conviction move mountains.

This is not a story of instant success. It's a story of slow miracles.

Of deportation and redirection.

Of sleeping on floors and standing in faith.

Of two broken legs that still couldn't stop this man from relentlessly running toward his destiny.

I have watched Adeola fall. I have also watched him rise again and again. Not for applause or accolades but because he carries a calling that is bigger than himself.

This book is not just about his journey. It's about yours.

Because somewhere inside every one of us is that same barefoot child hoping, hurting, reaching. And if you're holding this book, let me tell you: Your story isn't over, either.

What Adeola has built through the AOA Foundation—from the camp to the classroom, from Noble Court to every donated pair of shoes—goes beyond charity. He's built a legacy.

It is proof that prominence doesn't require polished beginnings. Greatness often grows out of the cracks, the very places we thought nothing good could come from.

So, I invite you to read these pages with more than your eyes. Read with your heart. Read with your soul open.

And read knowing that transformation is still within reach, for you, for your family, for your community.

By the time you reach the last page, I pray you ponder a new question: What will your footprints say when the concrete settles?

Because no matter where you start, you are called to leave a mark that lasts.

With all my heart,
Dr. Jackie Walters

Preface

I never set out to write a book. I set out to survive.

In the world I was born into, storytelling was a luxury we couldn't afford. Our mouths were too dry from hunger, our nights too short from worry, and our hands too full from trying to hold together what little we had. Words, when they came, were prayers. Soft, desperate prayers whispered between cracked lips and flickering lanterns. We didn't speak of dreams; we protected them. Like fragile embers, we cupped them with calloused hands and hoped the winds of poverty wouldn't blow them out.

Growing up in Nigeria, survival wasn't a figure of speech. It was a rhythm, a daily choreography of improvisation and endurance. I remember walking to school barefoot, the morning pavement already warm beneath my soles, each step a lesson in discomfort. Hunger accompanied us like a silent sibling, never speaking but always there. Some nights, I closed my eyes and imagined the sound of a full plate. On the hardest mornings, I pretended the water in my tin cup was *pap*,[1] and the air was thick with the imagined aroma of fried plantains.

My parents didn't have much, but what they could give us was sacred. My father, Idowu "ID Noble" Ajayi, set aside his own dreams so we might have the smallest chance at chasing ours. He could have been a renowned artist, painting the world as he saw it. Instead, he became a night watchman, painting our future with quiet sacrifice. My mother was a magician of miracles, from stretching two cups of rice into dinner for seven to folding brokenness into resilience. She didn't just hold our family together; she held up the sky.

---

1. A thick cornmeal porridge commonly eaten in West and South Africa.

This book isn't a highlight reel. There are no filters, no glossy cover to conceal the struggle. *Footprints on Concrete* is raw. It's the dirt under my toenails, the holes in my school shorts, the silence of a classroom when I had no lunch. It's also the sound of a basketball echoing off a crumbling court wall in Sango Ota—the first time I encountered my purpose.

I didn't write this story to prove that I've made it. I wrote it to prove that making it is possible.

For the barefoot child wondering if anyone even notices them: I see you.

For the teenager carrying invisible wounds and heavy expectations: I've been there.

For the young man or woman wondering if anything good can come from their village, their past, their pain: This book is your mirror.

This story is for the forgotten. The overlooked. The written-off.

It's a tribute, too—to those who didn't let me fall. To my late father, whose dignity fortified the foundation I now stand on. To my mother, whose strength was stitched into every meal she made and every prayer she whispered. To Coach Curtis Berry and Dr. Jackie Walters, whose open doors and open hearts became the home I never knew I needed. And to the children of Sango Ota, the heartbeat of the Adeola Ajayi Foundation: You are why I rise each day. Your laughter on Noble Court reminds me that pain doesn't have to get the final say.

And if you're holding this book, you're part of the story now, too—not just the one I've written but the one you assemble for yourself from these pages.

Because *Footprints on Concrete* isn't just a memoir. It's an invitation.

To believe again. To rise again.

To dream again.

Let it remind you that pain can become purpose. That broken roads can still lead to beautiful destinations. And that even if your path begins on concrete, you still have the power to leave footprints.

So, step forward.

And don't be afraid to make them deep.

—**Adeola Ajayi**

Acknowledgments

To God:

You were my whisper in the wilderness, my compass when I was lost in chaos.

My comfort when the nights stretched long and cold. When there was no food, You were the Bread.

When there was no way, You became the Path.

This story, this mission, the very breath I am taking—it all begins and ends with You.

This book is more than ink and paper.

It is the echo of answered prayers, the fruit of resilience, and the work of many unseen hands.

It is the result of *miracles*—some loud, others quiet—none of which I created alone.

To my late father, Idowu "ID Noble" Ajayi:

Your dreams may have been buried under the weight of sacrifice, but your spirit rose through me.

You laid down your brush so I could pick up my pen.

Noble Court is more than a namesake—it is a living altar to everything you gave up so that we could have more.

Every bounce of the ball there is a drumbeat in your honor.

Every child who plays beneath that sky is standing on the foundation you laid with your life.

I miss you. I honor you. I walk in your name.

To my mother, Mulikat Ajayi:

Mama, you were our lighthouse in the darkest storm.

You made magic from next to nothing—transforming onions and oil into nourishment, silence into strength.

You loved us through lack. You gave even when you had nothing left. You prayed over my destiny with cracked hands and sleepless nights.

I am the man I am today because you refused to break.

Thank you for teaching me that it's possible to survive and still love deeply.

To my siblings — Adebisi, Adeshola, Ademola, Adebola, and Adelola Akorede Ajayi:

We went through the fire together.

From our 9x9 room in Ebute Metta to where we stand now, you have been my inspiration and motivation since day one.

Thank you for enduring the heat, the hunger, and the heartache with me.

We shared more than space. We shared a dream we didn't yet have the words to express.

And we made it.

To my partner, Addy Kryger:

Thank you for being my backbone, my partner, and one of the brightest lights along this journey. Your heart, creativity, and tireless work have been instrumental to the growth of the AOA Foundation. From organizing every detail of the fundraising gala to standing beside me in the mess and the miracles, you've shown up with grace, strength, and vision. This book—and everything it represents—carries your fingerprints too.

To my sons, Elijah and Isaiah:

You are the living, breathing proof that hope endures.

Isaiah, your smile in the NICU, tethered to wires and surrounded by machines, reminded me what strength looks like.

Not loud. Not big. But stubborn. Holy. Defiant in the face of fear.

You are the continuation of a legacy born in dust and carried into destiny.

My love for you will build nations.

To Coach Peter Akindele:

You saw a skinny, barefoot boy with a fire in his eyes, and you didn't just walk past.

You gave me a ball, a direction, a purpose.

You planted a seed even though the soil was still dry and watered it with faith in the future. You didn't just coach me; you believed in me when I didn't know how to believe in myself.

Thank you for igniting the first spark.

To Coach Curtis Berry and Dr. Jackie Walters:

You opened your front door. More than that, you opened your hearts. You became my dad and mum, not by DNA but by decision.

You shielded me when I was vulnerable, disciplined me when I drifted, and loved me unconditionally.

Every time I lace up a pair of shoes for a child in Nigeria, I am mirroring the love you laced into my life.

You taught me that family is not just who you come from; it's who shows up.

To Ejike Ugboaja and Simon Akowe:

When the system said "no," when the door slammed shut on me and deportation loomed, you answered my cry.

Your kindness didn't just save a chapter of my life. It rewrote the entire story.

You didn't have to help me. But you did. And I will never forget it.

To Mark and Kelly Heiser:

You caught me when I had no place left to land and didn't ask for explanations. You simply said, "Come stay."

Your home became a sanctuary. Your kindness reminded me that restoration begins with being seen.

Thank you for giving me back my breath.

To Paul and Jen Elmore:

Your faith is gentle but fierce. Your service is quiet but seismic.

You showed me what it means to *be* the gospel—not just preach it.

Your lives are a sermon I carry with me.

To Jonathan Sever:

Thank you for being more than a mentor. Thank you for seeing something in me long before I saw it in myself. Your steady encouragement, your belief in my voice, and your persistent push to put my story on paper made this book.

You didn't just tell me I could do it. You walked with me through every doubt, every rewrite, every page. *Footprints on Concrete* would still be an untold story if not for you.

To Mr. Kunath, my high school art teacher:

You handed me a brush when I didn't even know how to hold onto a dream. You saw beauty in my pain and worth in my work. When you helped me apply to SCAD, you opened a door and pushed me toward the light.

Thank you for believing in my gift before I knew it was one.

To Emelyna Aurich—

The day I applied to work at One Light, all I wanted was to get out of the house and find something, anything, to keep me moving. I never could have imagined that that moment would lead to the opportunity of a lifetime. Now, more than six years later, I'm still here, and I'm still passionate about what I do.

Your leadership, support, and belief in me helped turn a simple job into a deeper meaning and profound purpose. Because of you, I have been able to grow in ways I never thought possible and found immense joy in putting smiles on our residents' faces every single day.

You didn't just offer me a role. You gave me a platform, a family, and the freedom to lead with heart. Your support has also been instrumental in the AOA Foundation's success, and I'll never forget how you've stood behind me since day one.

I am forever grateful.

To the AOA Foundation family:

Board members, volunteers, donors, and day-one believers, this movement breathes because of you. Together, we've served meals, distributed shoes, delivered hope, and built courts where none existed.

You went beyond supporting a mission. You made it real.

To the people of Sango Ota:

You are my beginning. My compass. My why.

Every court we paint, every camp we run, every bag of rice or hygiene kit we distribute—it's all for you.

May your children rise higher. May your laughter be louder. May your future be full.

To the Light KC community and my extended family across Kansas City and beyond:

You welcomed me as one of your own.

You gave me a platform, a purpose, and a place to serve.

You reminded me that home can be found, not just inherited. Thank you for embracing not just my mission but my heart.

And finally, to you, the reader:

To anyone who has ever felt forgotten.

To anyone whose pain has yet to find its purpose.

To anyone walking on cracked concrete, wondering if you matter...

This book is your proof that your story counts.

Your tears are not wasted.

Your beginnings, no matter how broken, still carry holy possibilities.

Concrete can crack. But dreams can still rise.

With every step, with every footprint, we move forward.

Together.

– Adeola Ajayi
AOA Foundation founder, author, dreamer, son of the soil

Prologue

I was five the first time I realized we were poor. Not because someone said it but because hunger screamed it.

That night, my stomach twisted and cried out like it was mourning something I couldn't name. Far from a soft ache, I felt a riot beneath my ribs, a protest I couldn't quell. We had no food, no light, and no promise that morning would bring anything better than the day before.

But beside me, my mother sat in the dark, humming a quiet song. Her voice was steady even when her world wasn't.

She rubbed my back with her tired hands, their palms callused from scrubbing clothes, from flipping yam slices over open flames, from lifting burdens too heavy for one woman alone.

Each stroke whispered the same truth: *You're still here. We still have breath. We still have a chance.*

That night, I clung to her humming like it was a lullaby woven from hope.

We lived in a 9x9 room in Ebute Metta, Lagos—not even one hundred square feet of space for my parents, my siblings, and all our possessions. Our clothes, our cookware, our secrets and stories. Yet our dreams refused to shrink, no matter how cramped the room became.

Rats danced in the ceiling. The roof leaked when the rains came. The cement floor was always cold, even when the heat outside begged for shade.

Under its shelter, we didn't just sleep side by side. We survived shoulder to shoulder, heartbeat to heartbeat.

I learned how to walk by stepping around potholes and puddles. I learned how to smile with cracked lips and an empty belly. I learned how to listen, from the silence when my father came home with his shoulders slumped once again to the tightness in my mother's voice when she stretched stew with water, praying we wouldn't notice.

But I learned something else, too. Something deeper than hunger or heat or humiliation.

I learned that suffering doesn't disqualify you. It prepares you.

It teaches you to be resourceful with broken things. To find beauty in the chipped corners of life. To dream anyway.

I didn't know it then, but my training had already begun. Not the kind that happens in gyms or schools, but the quiet kind that emerges in silence. In struggle. In shadows. The kind that builds something eternal in you: resilience.

Then one day, my older brother grabbed my hand and said, "Come."

He led me to a cracked concrete slab behind school—a so-called basketball court.

No net. One bent rim. Dust everywhere.

The kind of court rich schools refused to play on.

But to us, it was holy ground.

That first day, I stood barefoot on the concrete, the sun beating down like it had something to prove. My feet burned. My heart raced. I didn't know the rules. I didn't know the moves. I didn't even know the dream yet.

But the ball came to me. And I moved.

And in that moment—sweating, aching, unsure—I transformed.

The game gave me more than just something to do. It gave me something to *become*.

This book is about that barefoot boy. About how he became a man—not by skipping hardship but by walking through it. Sometimes crawling, sometimes crying, but always moving forward.

It's about what happens when pain becomes your teacher, when poverty becomes your podium, and when cracked concrete reveals your calling.

It's about the court that raised me and the people who caught me.

The faith that carried me.

And the legacy I am now laying, brick by brick, court by court, hand by hand.

This book isn't just about where I've been. It's about what can rise from those broken places.

It's about the footprints left behind—not just mine, but the ones you were made to leave, too.

So if you've ever walked through hard times…

If you've ever felt unseen, unheard, or unworthy…

If you've ever had a dream too big for your circumstances…

You belong here.

Because this story isn't mine alone. It's ours.

It's the story of what can rise from nothing. The story of *Footprints on Concrete*.

Now turn the page.

And let the journey begin.

Welcome

I was born into a world that didn't make room for dreamers.

Not in the way the world romanticizes dreams—with soft pillows and bright futures—but in a place where dreaming was a quiet act of rebellion, a gossamer hope whispered in the dark.

My earliest memories come from a 9x9 room in Ebute Metta, Lagos, a space so small that every breath we took had to save space for someone else's. My siblings and I slept like puzzle pieces—six bodies sharing one mat, elbows in ribs, feet in faces, hearts pounding beneath the same cracked ceiling. The walls were thin, but the silence was thick—the kind of silence that grows in homes where the parents love deeply, but the cupboards echo empty.

My father, Idowu Ajayi—known around the neighborhood as ID Noble—was an artist, a man whose hands were meant to paint beauty into this world. But life had other plans. In our part of the city, dreams didn't pay rent.

So, he laid his brush down and picked up a nightstick. He became a security guard, trading color and canvas for a uniform and long shifts under flickering bulbs. He never complained. But I could see it in his eyes: the quiet mourning of a gift unfulfilled.

My mother—my iron-spined mother—was the epitome of grace and grit. She made miracles out of onions and palm oil, turned handfuls of rice into meals for six, and fasted without ever calling it a sacrifice. She carried exhaustion like jewelry, elegant and unbreakable. She prayed over our heads in the morning and kissed our foreheads at night, always whispering, "You are more than this."

We shared everything. Not just food or hand-me-downs but dreams, too—the rare and precious kind we didn't dare speak aloud.

Because in that neighborhood, dreaming felt dangerous. Like tempting fate. Like asking for too much.

For much of my childhood, I walked barefoot—not just to school or church or pickup games in dusty lots but through life itself. The soles of my feet grew calloused, but so did my resolve. Every step was a promise: *You may not have much, but you have movement. You have momentum. Keep going.*

This book is not just about basketball.

It's not just about crossing oceans, surviving hardship, or building something from scratch.

It's about what happens when life knocks the very breath out of you, and you choose to get up anyway.

About what happens when the world turns cold, and you decide to keep your heart warm.

It's about the hunger that builds urgency. Vision.

This is a story about faith—the kind that doesn't shout from the rooftops but whispers into empty rooms, *Keep going.*

About resilience—the kind forged in scarcity, not comfort. In silence. In sweat.

About people—the ones who cracked open locked doors, gave me shelter when I was nearly homeless, answered desperate midnight pleas, and believed in me before I knew how to believe in myself.

It's about the boy who was kicked out of school and deposited on a plane with a one-way ticket and no plan.

The boy who broke both legs but kept running.

The boy who missed meals, flights, and opportunities—but never missed the chance to try again.

The father who nearly lost his own son at birth, then found his late father's spirit reflected in a tiny smile in the NICU.

It's about Noble Court—the community space I built in Sango Ota, Nigeria—poured with cement and love, painted with pride, and engraved with the names of the giants who carried me there. A court built not just for games but for the generations to come.

It's about the AOA Foundation, born from pain but rooted in purpose.

Born from a barefoot boy's whisper: *"There has to be more than this."* Cultivated into a movement that feeds, teaches, and uplifts hundreds of children. That nourishes young spirits who remind me of who I was and who they could become.

Footprints on Concrete is my story. But it's not mine alone.

Because if you're holding this book, then you've become part of it, too.

Every word is a footprint, every chapter a step. All toward something greater.

So, whether you've walked cracked streets like mine or just wondered how to rise when life feels too heavy, this book is for you. It's about where I've been and about where we go from here. Together.

For their futures. For your purpose. For the legacy still unwritten.

Let's begin.

Part One

The Struggle

1

Where It All Began

Love, Struggle, and the Invisible Weight of Poverty

Before I ever touched a basketball, before the thought of America even flickered in my imagination, I was just a boy trying to breathe inside a box we called home.

No. 2 Lagos Street, Ebute Metta, was a living, breathing being—wheezing with rust, layered in stories, sweat, and the unrelenting sun. Our little room sat on the second floor of a building that leaned like an old man whose tired bones still stood defiantly amid the chaos of Lagos. It was the same home my father had grown up in. I never met his parents, but I felt them in the walls, in every crack and every faded picture that clung to the concrete like it was afraid to let go.

Six of us fit inside that space: my parents, my siblings, and me. No hall. No door to close. Just walls, a thin mattress, and what little we owned stacked in the corners. Our entire world fit within that square. There was no privacy—not even in sadness. Every tear had witnesses. Every hunger pang had echoes.

And yet we loved. We laughed.

We survived.

The Street That Never Slept

From our only window, the city screamed.

Outside, Muritala Mohammed Way pulsed with sound—a symphony of honking *danfos*,[2] shouting hawkers, and clanging metal resonating from the Oyingbo Market. The smell of burning petrol drifted in from the station nearby, mixed with the sharp fragrance of frying pepper and the acidic smoke of burning waste. It clung to our clothes, our hair, our lungs. Every inhale was a reminder: You are still here.

You are still fighting.

Every morning, the sun arrived like a thief, sneaking in between the wooden slats to paint stripes on our skin. We woke not to alarms but to the sounds of life stirring outside and the silent prayers of a mother already up, wondering how to stretch one meal into three.

My Father's Paint-Stained Hands

My father was a man who once dreamed in color, an artist in both title and soul. His fingers told stories better than his lips ever could. Paintbrush in hand, he created worlds more vivid than our own, bringing to life women wrapped in *Ankara*,[3] the streets of Lagos soaked in twilight, boys flying kites in alleys where real birds were too hungry to soar. His work was brilliant. Alive.

But Lagos does not always reward brilliance. It tests it. Buries it. Forces it to make sacrifices.

I remember the mornings I'd rise to the smell of turpentine and kerosene and find him sitting cross-legged, lost in his canvas. The world could be crumbling, but in that moment, he was somewhere else.

And I'd go with him.

We walked side by side through the heat, carrying his artwork to galleries, hoping—begging, even—that someone else would recognize what I already knew: that my father was gifted.

Once, he sold a stunning portrait that had taken him weeks to finish for a fraction of its worth. We needed the money. But when we passed the

---
2. Taxis.
3. Colorful garments made from a vibrant, patterned cotton fabric. Also known as African wax print.

gallery days later and saw the same painting on display for ten times the price, something broke in me.

"It's not fair," I said.

My father looked at me with tired eyes and replied, "But we will eat tonight, won't we?"

That was his power: turning defeat into dignity.

Eventually, though, his paintbrush could no longer feed us. He took a job as a night security guard. Flashlight in hand, he guarded the kind of wealth we would never touch. He stood in the shadows so we could have light. And he never once complained.

My Mother, the Engineer of Miracles

If my father was the soul, my mother, Mulikat, was the fire. She didn't rest; she roared. She hawked boiled rice at dawn, sold cloth at noon, fetched water and sold it in jerry cans by evening. Whatever she could carry, she sold. And whatever she made, she stretched like magic.

On nights when food was short, she ate last—or not at all. I remember watching her stir broth made from bones, humming softly, pretending it was just the way she liked it.

Christmas was the hardest. In Lagos, Christmas is sacred. The streets explode with color—new clothes, toys, food, laughter. But for us, there was no budget for "new." So, my mother would rummage through her old wrappers—vibrant fabrics from her younger days—and take them to a tailor. We stepped out in repurposed glory, heads held high, as if the outfits had come straight from a boutique. She gave us dignity stitched with sacrifice.

She never asked for thanks, but every fiber of our survival was sewn by her hands.

Nights on the Floor

We slept packed tight, like books on a shelf, on one thin mattress where the springs poked through like stubborn weeds. Sometimes, we had to flip it over and air it outside, hoping it wouldn't fall apart. When the rainy season came and the ceiling leaked, we caught droplets with bowls and prayed it wouldn't pour harder.

The nights without electricity were long and quiet. We lit kerosene lanterns and watched the smoke etch lines in the air like ghosts. When the power came on, even for five minutes, we cheered like we'd won the lottery. But most nights, it was just us and the flickering flame casting our dreams against the peeling walls.

And somehow, we felt safe.

That room may have been small, but the love inside made it bigger than any mansion.

Poverty With a Heavy Voice

Poverty isn't just about lack. It's about weight.

It settles on your chest. It makes decisions for you. It whispers doubts when you try to dream.

At Ago Egba Primary School, I wore a shirt that used to be white but had faded to the color of old paper. My shorts had more patches than fabric. Some days, I was sent home because of torn clothing or no shoes. Most days, I walked barefoot, feeling the sting of hot asphalt, the gravel carving cuts into my soles, the shame of being "the boy with no shoes."

Yet I still went. I borrowed notes. I read by lantern light. I studied hard, desperate to climb out.

Some days, I'd come home and find nothing. No food. No water. Just silence. My mother would scrape together a few meager coins, just enough to buy a single plate of *Eba*[4] and stew. She'd add water to the stew, magically making more. And that one piece of meat? She'd cut it in six, one bite for each of us.

We called it dinner. We called it love.

---

4. A stiff, cooked dough made from cassava flour, often served with soup or sauce.

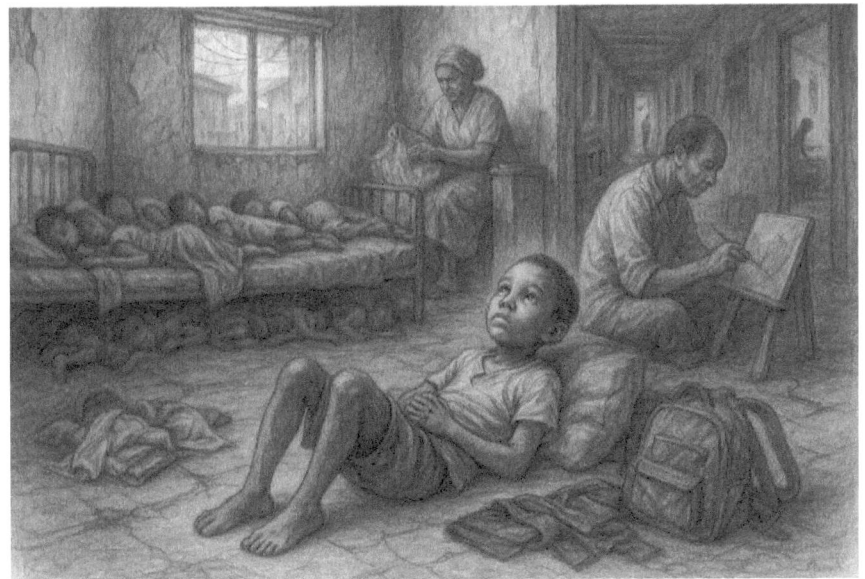

2

Growing Up in Lagos

Tightness

The clash between dreams and daily hunger. School in torn uniforms. Walking barefoot. Eviction looming.

I don't remember every detail of my early childhood, but I remember the feeling: tightness.

It became a way of life, from the walls of our one-room apartment pressing in, the heat and hopelessness looming over us, to the silence of hunger hanging in the air, thick and unmoving. No one had the strength to speak, not even to complain. My siblings and I lay shoulder to shoulder on a shared mat, our spines digging into the cracked concrete floor, our bodies twisted together like the threads of a worn-out rope.

Our stomachs tightened, too, after days when water was our only meal. And we drank it slowly, savoring the lie it told—that we were full.

That tightness never really left me. Even today, I feel it sometimes, a quiet pressure under my ribs like a reminder from the past. It taught me early how fragile life can be, how quickly comfort can vanish. How you can fall—and keep falling—and the world will keep turning like nothing's happened.

And yet, in that space of hunger, another thing took root.

Awareness.

I noticed everything. The trembling in my mother's hands as she measured out uncooked rice, trying to divide hope evenly between bowls. The hesitation in my father's eyes before answering questions about money, as though speaking of it might break what little pride he had left. I saw how other children—well-fed, well-dressed—moved through life like it owed them something.

But for us, life owed nothing. We were forced to snatch up whatever scraps we could, not out of bitterness but necessity.

The Window to Another Life

Our 9x9 room had just one window. And from that window, I watched another world pass by, one I didn't belong to.

Children walked to school in clean white shirts tucked neatly into precisely ironed shorts. Their socks were high. Their shoes clicked proudly against the ground like punctuation marks to their privilege. They laughed freely, the kind of laughter that had never known an empty stomach.

I didn't hate them. I envied them.

But it wasn't jealousy. It was longing. I longed to have what they did, too. I longed for things that were so simple but always so out of reach. A full meal. Unpatched shorts. Shoes that didn't talk when you walked.

When I did have shoes, they were held together with thread, tape, and willpower. When they finally gave out, I had no choice but to walk barefoot on the merciless Lagos pavement. The heat burned into my soles. Every stone was a test of my willpower. I learned to walk on the outer edges of my feet just to give the blisters time to heal. My toes were covered in calluses. But I kept walking.

Because hunger couldn't be an excuse to stop.

Because even in shame, school was still school. And I had dreams too.

Mornings Without Breakfast

We woke up early, but not because we were disciplined. Our sleep was simply never deep enough to carry us past dawn. Hunger has a way of nudging you before the sun does.

My mother, always the first to rise, would light the coal pot in the corner. The smoke would wrap itself around our room, soaking into every inch of wall and fabric. If we were lucky, she'd make *pap*, cornmeal boiled into a watery paste. If we were luckier, there'd be a handful of rice or a bit of soaked *garri*.

But most mornings, there was nothing. Just water.

We drank it like it could sustain us, like it could fool our stomachs into silence. We brushed our teeth with no paste. We dressed in uniforms stiff from being washed without soap. Then we walked to school, heads high, faces hollow, pretending we were just like every other kid.

And my mother, no matter how tired or defeated she looked, would reheat the same pot of stew every morning. No fridge meant no choice. That stew had to survive the week.

She guarded it like treasure. Added water to stretch it, salt to trick the tongue. Meat was rare, and what little we had was more bone than flesh.

But it was warm.

And warmth was something.

The Village Visit—A New Kind of Hard

Every now and then, we left Lagos to visit my grandmother, Iya Ibadan, in Ilepa, a village tucked between Sango Ota and Ifo in Ogun State. I thought I knew struggle, but Ilepa introduced me to a different kind.

The routine there was unlike anything I had known. Each morning began with a gulp of *Agbo*, a local herbal remedy my grandmother brewed from bitter leaves and roots.

She believed it kept us healthy. I believed it was the worst part of our childhood.

The acrid taste hit the tongue like a punishment—sharp, earthy, cruel—and lingered long after.

We lined up barefoot with our plastic plates, waiting for food. In cities, some children had bread and eggs. In Ilepa, we had *Eba* pressed from cassava flour, most times with no meat. It was just a watery soup, maybe with mushrooms on a good day. Mushrooms were the protein of the poor.

And after eating, we walked to the farm.

It was at least 1.5 hours away, sometimes two. Barefoot, we waded through five rivers. Cold water, sharp rocks, thorns, leeches—all just part of the path. We left early, before the sun woke fully. No conversation, just walking. The air was always thick with dew, and the mist clung to our legs like spectral fingers.

My grandmother didn't own a farm. She worked on others' farms for money or a portion of cassava. And her grandchildren helped. We uprooted cassava, our tiny hands pulling against roots anchored deep in the soil. Sometimes, we carried firewood or fetched water. Always, we worked.

When we finished digging up the cassava, we tied it in sacks and placed it on our heads. That was the test.

If you cried that it was too heavy, the workers would laugh and take some out.

But I didn't want to cry. I wanted to be strong. So I carried it.

The pressure on my neck felt like someone tightening a belt around my throat. My legs trembled. My arms ached. Eventually, I'd drop it by the side of the road, rest, and wait. Someone older would walk back and help me lift it again.

I couldn't do it alone. But I tried.

Bruises That Wouldn't Heal

On one visit, I arrived with wounds.

I had fallen back in Lagos, scraping up my legs and losing a toenail. But we had no money for bandages. No antiseptic. Just open wounds and the will to keep moving.

In Ilepa, there was no mercy for the injured.

I still had to walk, farm, fetch water.

We crossed the same rivers. Amid the muddy waters, my infected toe stung with each step, each splash a spasm of fire. There was no rest or healing.

The wound festered, staying open for more than a month.

But nothing and no one paused. Not life, not hunger.

We ate *Eba* in the morning, *garri* with peanuts in the afternoon, and *Eba* again at night. Every meal felt like déjà vu. But we were grateful.

Because at least we had something.

The Seed Beneath the Struggle

It was during those long walks, those hungry mornings, those painful steps that something else was planted: conviction.

Even in the emptiness, I began to dream. I began to believe—truly believe—that one day, I'd tell this story from a different place. And I would tell it not with bitterness but with purpose.

Because every blister, every skipped meal, every river crossed with unprotected feet was shaping me. I didn't know how or when or what would come. But those nights in Ilepa, as mosquitoes droned around my head and my toe throbbed with pain, I lay under the stars and whispered, "There has to be more than this."

And I held on to that hope like the last breath before a deep plunge.

3

The Classroom

I went to Ago Egba Primary School, where "school" meant something entirely different than what most people imagine.

There were no ceiling fans. No electricity. Not even windows—just holes in the walls where air should have passed through but didn't.

When the sun rose, the stagnant heat came with it—heavy, stubborn, and suffocating. It choked the room like smoke. By mid-morning, sweat glued our shirts to our backs. The walls absorbed the heat and then breathed it back like a furnace. The air inside the classroom was so thick, it felt like trying to breathe through cotton.

And still we showed up.

Cramped Spaces, Open Minds

More than forty children squeezed into rooms meant to fit twenty. Some sat on rickety benches, and others knelt on the floor or leaned against the wall. Most shared torn notebooks. The concrete was cracked, and so was the roof. When it rained, the storm didn't just knock on the door: It came in uninvited.

With no windows to shut and no glass to shield us, the rain blasted through the hollows in the wall. Cold water splashed onto our desks, soaked our notebooks, and left puddles at our feet. We huddled in corners, trying to protect our only materials from ruin, our knees drawn to our chests like we could fold ourselves away from the wetness.

The chalkboard was barely usable, its surface scratched to a dull gray. Most days, the teacher wrote with chalk so small that it had to be pinched like a needle. The letters barely left a mark. But we leaned forward and squinted anyway, desperate to capture any knowledge we could.

The Uniform of Poverty

Our uniforms were more symbol than fabric. My khaki shorts were soft from wear. Their seams threatened to split if I stretched too far. My once-white shirt had faded to the dull hue of old paper, stained and collarless. There were days when the fabric barely held together.

I didn't own a school bag. Instead, I tied my books together with old rubber bands and carried them in my hands or under my arm. I had inherited them all from siblings and neighbors, their pages already full of someone else's handwriting and dreams.

Then, one day, the government came to hand out new books. Clean, fresh, never even opened. I still remember the smell—sharp as a promise. I meticulously wrapped my new treasure in old newspapers, folding the edges with care, guarding them like sacred scripture. That book became my most prized possession—not because of the knowledge inside but because of what it meant: Someone believed I was worth all these pages.

Burning Light and Flickering Hope

I wasn't the smartest student in the class. But I may have been the most determined.

I borrowed notes. I copied my classmates' assignments word for word. I stayed behind after school, asking questions others were too afraid or too proud to ask. They laughed. I didn't care.

I wasn't chasing grades. I was chasing escape.

At night, I studied by kerosene lantern. Our home had no electricity—just the soft, trembling flame of a lantern, its smoke curling into the air like fingers. The light danced across my book, too dim to make out the words. I had to hold them just inches away, blinking through the sting in my eyes as I strained to see.

My stomach growled. My head throbbed. Through it all, I read, convinced that maybe—just maybe—if I could outlearn my reality, I could outrun it, too.

The Streets: My After-School Freedom

When the school day ended, I ran to the streets—not to escape danger, but to find a piece of freedom.

The streets of Lagos were loud and unforgiving, but they didn't judge. They didn't care if I was poor or barefoot. They only asked one thing: *Show up.*

We played soccer with balls jerry-rigged from rags and plastic bags, wrapped tightly and tied with twine. Our goalposts were sticks. Our field was a strip of dirt behind the mechanic's shop. But we shouted like we were in a crowded stadium. Our feet bled. Our laughter soared.

Between games, I carried water for neighbors, swept doorsteps, ran errands for small change, a biscuit, sometimes nothing more than a nod. Just acknowledgment. And still I persisted.

Because survival isn't just about food: It's about motion. Momentum. It's about staying stubbornly visible in a world trying to forget you.

A Need to Belong

What I wanted more than anything was to belong—to feel chosen, needed, part of something structured and proud.

That was why I joined the Boys Brigade at a nearby African church. They wore white uniforms and marched in formation, beating drums and singing songs. I practiced the rhythms, rehearsed the steps, memorized the lines. I was ready for Palm Sunday.

But the day before the parade, I was told I couldn't march. I didn't have the right uniform.

No white shirt. No white pants. No socks. No tennis shoes. No spot.

I stood in the shadows as the others passed by, their drums echoing down the street. I clapped. Smiled, even.

But deep inside, I cracked.

Because that day, I learned a truth that cuts deeper than hunger: that poverty doesn't just take what's in your pocket. It takes your invitation to the table. It makes you invisible. It keeps you forever watching, never participating.

Hunger: The First Teacher

I had many teachers. But hunger was my first and most persistent.

It taught me patience—how to wait without asking.

It taught me creativity—how to chew slowly, drink water like it was sustenance, and smile when classmates brought out lunches I could never afford.

It taught me to treasure crumbs like blessings and to find joy in even the smallest victories: a cold sachet of water, a shared slice of bread, a single boiled egg split between siblings.

It taught me not to expect but to endure.

The Day the Floor Dropped

The day my childhood ended, my father came home early—something he never did. His face was set in stone, but his eyes betrayed the truth before his mouth even moved.

Our building had been sold.

We had thirty days to leave. No appeals, no mercy. The landlord had simply ended everything we knew with a single sentence.

My mother's silent stare as she sank slowly to the floor told me everything I needed to know.

The fear was instant. We had no savings and no one to call. No idea where we'd go next. No backup plan. Just faith.

We packed our entire lives into raffia[5] bags. A few clothes. Cookware. My father's paintbrushes. My mother's headwraps. The radio. My wrapped-up schoolbooks. That's all we had.

We boarded a crowded *danfo* bus. I sat by the window and watched Lagos disappear behind me. The buildings. The corners I used to play on. The people I knew. All of it slipped into memory.

---

5. Strong, durable tote bags crafted from the fibers of a raffia palm tree.

I wasn't just leaving a city.

I was leaving behind a version of myself.

We headed away from Lagos, away from everything familiar, to Sango Ota, Ogun State. A smaller city, a slower pace. It felt like exile.

No more school. No more friends. No more knowing where I was or who I was becoming.

But the tears didn't come. I just stared out the window and felt the ground fall away.

As the bus bounced down the dusty road and our future lay shrouded in doubt, I whispered to myself, "This is not where the story ends."

Because even with nothing in my hands, even with the tightness in my chest and the clamor of poverty still ringing in my ears, I still clutched onto one unshakable belief: that there had to be more than this.

And somehow, some way, I was going to find it.

20 | The Classroom

4

Barefoot Dreams

A Different Kind of Struggle

Moving to Sango Ota was like falling through the cracks of life.

Lagos had been chaos, yes—loud, dirty, fast—but it had rhythm. Energy. Momentum.

Sango Ota, on the other hand, was still. Too still, like a heart that had neglected its next beat. The day we arrived, it felt like the air itself had forgotten how to move.

We came with nothing but raffia bags, plastic buckets, and the heavy silence of people who had no other choice. I remember stepping off the danfo, my feet sinking into the unfamiliar dust, my eyes searching for anything that resembled a future.

But all I saw was sheer destitution, stripped of all pretense.

A New Standard of Living

Our life in Lagos had been rife with hardships. But our new compound on Ojubanire Close was worse.

We moved into a 9x9 room in a face-me-I-face-you[6] compound, long and narrow, with ten rooms mirroring each other across a corridor that served

---

6. A style of apartment in Nigeria in which the entrances of one- or two-room apartments face each other along a long hallway leading to the main entrance, typically rented to low-income families.

as both community and battlefield. You could walk the length of the entire compound in twenty steps. Each door opened into a family's entire world. There were no secrets, no silence, and absolutely no privacy.

The walls were thin—sometimes just partitions of plywood nailed together with hope. Conversations, arguments, births, and grief all spilled into one another. The baby crying in Room 3 was everyone's baby. The fight in Room 7 was a play performed for the entire corridor. Laughter, weeping, prayers—they all echoed, always.

The bathrooms were not bathrooms in any modern sense, just cement corners with holes in the floor. No doors, sinks, or any semblance of dignity. Some people tried hanging rice sack curtains for privacy. Others didn't bother.

And when it rained, the water poured through the roof like it was made of paper. Water mingled with waste. Puddles gathered like reminders that suffering had layers.

And yet we adapted. We had no choice.

We bathed with buckets. When the soap ran out, we scrubbed ourselves with powdered detergent that stung like fire. We prayed the toilets wouldn't collapse.

As a boy, I often stood in the open wash stall, my back to the world, trying to hide the way my ribs peeked through my skin. I tried to be quick, invisible. But you can't hide your hunger from water. It reflects you back—stripped and raw.

Hawking Hope

My mother—God bless the fire in her bones—refused to let hunger win.

She had no money to start a business, but she had hustle. She would go to the market and borrow goods on credit—fruits, vegetables, leafy greens, whatever was in season. She never begged. She negotiated with dignity. "I'll pay you when we sell," she'd say in a tone so confident that even debt sounded like a promise.

She came home balancing baskets filled with okra, bitter leaf, mangoes, oranges, and garden eggs. Sometimes the produce came wrapped in old newspapers or poured into tattered black nylon bags. She'd divide them carefully, pack them onto aluminum trays, and assign one to each of us.

One for my brother, one for me.

She would cushion the tray on my head with a ring of cloth, adjust it with both hands, then look me in the eye and whisper, "Sell well, my son. God is with you."

We hawked from dawn until the sun grew angry, rambling along dirt roads and cracked tar. Our feet danced around potholes and sewage, sometimes sinking in mud, sometimes kicking up dust.

We called out with practiced songs: "Oraaaange! Sweet orange! Fresh orange-o!" "Tomato! Tomato! Very red! Very sweet!" "Buy your *ugu*[7]! Fresh *ugu* leaves here!"

I made sales and had my regulars—women who liked my voice, who smiled when I joked. Some would buy more just to help. Some would even give me cold water or a banana. Their kindness wasn't pity. It was recognition. They saw me for who I was: just a boy pretending to be a man.

And when I returned home with an empty tray and naira[8] notes folded tight in my palm, Mama would take the money and nod slowly, tears hiding in her eyes.

"You're your father's son," she'd say. "You know how to sell. You have the gift."

Those were the few moments when she allowed herself joy.

Roaches, Rats, and Resilience

In Sango Ota, home wasn't a refuge. It was a battlefield.

Cockroaches ruled the night, slipping through cracks and skittering across pots and pans. We covered our food not to preserve it but to defend it. Rats chewed through our bags and shared our floor. Once, one even bit my heel as I slept. The pain startled me awake, and the blood that followed left a scar I still carry on both my foot and my memory.

Mosquitoes buzzed like pestilent lullabies. We didn't have nets, just old wrappers draped across our bodies like tissue-thin shields. They bit us anyway.

---

7. Fluted pumpkin. This popular vegetable's nutritious leaves are a staple ingredient in many African dishes.
8. Nigerian currency. As of this book's publication, the exchange rate is approximately 1,600 naira to one U.S. dollar. One naira is divided into 100 kobo.

Malaria was a season, not a disease. It came and went like harmattan[9]—predictable and punishing. We didn't have any money for hospitals. Instead, we drank bitter *Agbo*, letting it burn our throats as it went down. We sweated through fevers, shivered through chills, and prayed that we would not become mere stories.

Electricity was rare. Most nights, we sat in darkness, our tiny home lit only by a flickering kerosene lantern. When the silence settled in, the mosquitoes came alive. They buzzed in our ears with that maddening, high-pitched whine that's impossible to ignore. We slapped ourselves raw trying to kill them. If we were lucky, we'd catch a fat one, bloated from our blood and flying slow. Kill one, and the blood would splatter across your face, proof that you'd won one tiny battle in a losing war.

Roaches took the night shift.

They emerged like phantoms—red ones, black ones, thick brown ones with twitching legs. Males, females, babies, queens. They'd scurry across the room, fly across your face, crawl into crevices, sometimes even into our food. We tried to keep them out, but hunger doesn't wait for perfect conditions.

One night, my mother had been slow-cooking a pot of *egusi*[10] soup over three days, stretching every ingredient with water and prayer. That night, we finally sat down to eat. No electricity, just the lantern's warm, trembling glow. I dipped my *Eba* into the pot and felt something firm. Textured. Like meat. Fish? Maybe shrimp?

My heart leaped—extra protein, a gift from God. I sucked it, savoring the richness.

Then, something told me to check.

I pulled it out of my mouth, walked slowly to the lantern, and held it under the light.

A cockroach.

Large. Brown. Female. It blended so well with the soup that it could've passed for beef. My stomach turned. I gagged, spat, nearly vomited.

I didn't eat that night. I couldn't.

---

9. A season from late November to early March in which an especially dry, dusty easterly wind blows from the Sahara along the West African coast.
10. Ground melon seed.

But my mother just looked at me and said softly, "It's okay. You don't have to. Tomorrow will come."

And she kept eating. Because mothers don't always get the luxury of refusal.

The Perfume of Poverty

There are places you remember not just by how they looked but by how they smelled. How they itched. How they sounded when the lights were out and survival was your lullaby. For us, that place was our room in Sango Ota.

Our space was no larger than a prison cell, yet it contained a world—six souls, one mattress, and an unrelenting swarm of uninvited guests. We didn't just share the room with each other. We shared it with rats that chewed through walls, cockroaches that flew like miniature helicopters in the dark, mosquitoes that sang into our ears, and bed bugs that made our skin their playground.

Every morning, we woke up itching, scratching, blistered. Red rashes lined our arms, backs, and necks. We'd look at each other, eyes puffy with fatigue, and silently ask: *What war did we fight in our sleep?*

My mother never needed to ask. She knew.

She'd lift the corner of our wafer-thin, sunken mattress—always at the edge, always at the seams—and like clockwork, the kingdom revealed itself.

Bed bugs. Dozens. Hundreds. Scattering like thieves at the break of dawn. My mother would clench her jaw and press her thumb against them—*pop, pop, pop*—each bursting with blood.

But not their blood. Ours. Mine. My sister's. My baby brother's.

The blood of her children, stolen in the night.

And the smell...

God, the *smell*.

To this day, I still remember it.

A rancid, metallic, musty stench, somewhere between rust and rot, something primal and sour. The smell of filth and fear, of skin and sweat and decay all mingled in one.

It clings to the back of your throat like smoke. And once you've smelled it, you never forget.

To this day, I know when bed bugs are present. Even in the most luxurious room, the swankiest hotel, the moment I catch even a trace of that smell, my body remembers. My skin crawls. My mind goes back to that room. That mattress. That kingdom.

My mother would drag the mattress outside, douse it in kerosene—the same kerosene we used to cook—and lay it out under the sun. The fumes rose in thick waves. The next night, we'd lie down and inhale that kerosene all through our sleep. Our noses burned. Our eyes watered. But the bed bugs were gone—at least for a night or two.

This Was Our Life

Poverty isn't just a lack of money.

It's sharing your room with kingdoms of infestation. It's having no choice but to eat what may kill you. It's scratching until you bleed. It's the blood-and-kerosene stench of your childhood. It's watching your mother do battle with her bare hands while the world sleeps.

We lived with shame, hunger, and creatures that thrived in our darkness. But somehow, we also lived with hope.

The Lesson in the Infestation

That room taught me how to endure. Not in theory but in bone.

I learned that discomfort does not destroy you. It shapes you.

That survival is not weakness—it's training.

That your current condition does not determine your final identity.

I learned to dream beyond the infestation.

And I promised myself that, someday, my children would not have to live like this.

That promise became Noble Court. That memory became my mission.

Because when you've slept with a kingdom of parasites, you learn to build sanctuaries for others. You learn to tell the roaches from the blessings.

You learn to smell danger before it arrives.

Now, I walk in clean rooms. I lay my children on soft mattresses. I travel the world. But a single scent can transport me back. The boy who shared his sleep with rats, roaches, bed bugs, and mosquitoes—he still walks with me.

And every court I build, every mattress I donate, every meal I serve…It's not just for him.

It's for the millions of children still scratching in the dark, still learning what resilience smells like.

The Room That Held Everything

Our room held everything we owned and everything we dreamed of.

One crooked cupboard with peeling paint stored our pots, plates, and sense of order. My father's old easel stood in a corner, its legs wobbling, its canvas blank. He hadn't painted in years. That part of him had been swallowed by bills, late shifts as a guard, by the long hours spent standing under fluorescent lights that weren't his.

There was also a locked wooden cabinet, small and mysterious. We never knew what was inside. As kids, we whispered about it like it held treasure or tickets out of poverty. Maybe it did. Or maybe it just held memories our parents were too tired to look at.

My parents had a bed—worn, creaky, bowed in the middle. We slept on mats on the floor, shoulder to shoulder, back to back, rotating positions as we fought for space. When it rained, the leaks turned the floor into a puddle. We moved like swimmers through sleep, dodging the drops with drowsy precision.

There was no wardrobe. Our clothes lived in black nylon bags, knotted tightly and stacked against the wall. Some we hung from nails. Others we laid out to dry, praying the sun would come before mold did.

Heat, Hunger, and Hope

The heat in Sango Ota wasn't heat—it was retribution.

The tin roof boiled us. The air didn't move. The room became an oven, and we were the bread left inside a little too long. Electricity was only a rumor:

It came rarely and never stayed. When it did, we shouted, clapped, danced. We plugged in anything with a cord, whether it needed charging or not.

Water was rationed. Soap was stretched. Dreams were folded and stored for later.

And still we dreamed.

The Dream That Refused to Die

I dreamed of more. Not luxury or comfort, just change.

I dreamed of handing my mother a key, saying, "No more rent. No more moving. This is yours."

I dreamed of flying—*really* flying—of sitting on a plane, watching the clouds roll beneath me, whispering to myself, "We made it."

And what was wild was that I didn't just wish it. I believed it. Even when my feet were blistered from hawking. Even when I lay on a mat soaked with sweat. Even when rats bit, mosquitoes feasted, and the world forgot us, I believed.

Because poverty could take my comfort but not my calling.

It could silence the house but not my hope.

Somewhere ahead, I knew a moment was coming. A court. A game. A chance.

And I promised myself I would be ready.

Joy in the Shadows

Even there, in the shadow of struggle, joy snuck in.

We made balls out of plastic bags and rags. We used sticks as goalposts. Our cheers echoed across the dust. We laughed under the moon. We raced through the alleys barefoot and built dreams out of dirt.

We didn't know we were poor. We only knew we were alive.

Sango Ota tested me.

It broke me.

And it built me.

Life there taught me that survival is a skill and grit is a muscle. I learned that even when you have nothing, you can still choose to hope.

One night, I lay on the floor, my stomach empty but my heart full. Amid the quiet, I whispered into the dark, "There has to be more than this."

And that night, I made a promise: I would find it.

5

The Day My Brother Dragged Me to School III

Soccer Was My First Love

Before basketball ever found me, I was in love with soccer.

In Nigeria, soccer is more than a pastime. It's a birthright. It's the anthem of the streets—a language spoken in bruises and barefoot goals, in cheers that rise like smoke from alleyways and sandlots. If it rolled, we kicked it. If it bounced, we chased it.

Our balls were made of anything but leather. Tied-up plastic bags, rolled-up socks, crushed cans. Here, real balls were only a myth. But we played like champions anyway, scraping our toes raw on rough concrete as we dove for headers on unpadded ground. The dust of Joju was our stadium, and we played until the orange sky dissolved into night.

I remember mimicking Jay-Jay Okocha's flicks, pretending to dribble like Kanu, the legendary long-legged magician. I'd juggle barefoot, dodge imaginary defenders, hear the stadium in my head roar with every move.

We didn't have cleats. We didn't need them; we had dreams.

But passion doesn't always promise escape. None of the boys I knew—at least, none from families like mine—had made it. But we chased the ball anyway because it gave us what hunger couldn't: joy, identity, belonging.

Then one afternoon, the game changed—not because of a ball but because of my brother's voice.

"Come With Me"

My older brother, Adeshola, was always the quiet one. He didn't talk much, but when he did, his words carried weight.

"Come with me to School III," he said one dry afternoon. "There's a coach starting a basketball team. I think you'll like it."

I stared at him.

Basketball? That was the game on TV with tall Americans, shiny floors, and rules that made no sense to me. It didn't live in our neighborhood. I'd never touched a real basketball. I didn't even know anyone who played. I laughed.

"Basketball *ke*? *Abeg*, leave me *jor*."

But Adeshola was persistent. He didn't argue, but he also didn't stop asking. Every day.

"Let's go," he'd say. "Just try it."

Maybe he saw something in me before I did. Maybe he was just trying to pull me from routine. But after enough nagging, I finally gave in.

School III

We walked through Joju, the sun baking the red sand into our skin, our feet kicking up dust with every step. The roads were cracked. The gutters reeked. Sweat slid down my spine. And when we finally arrived at School III, I thought, *This? This is it?*

It didn't look like a court. It looked like a graveyard for forgotten dreams.

The concrete was chipped, broken in places. The rim had no net and leaned to the side like it was tired of waiting. The backboard looked like it would crumble if you prodded it too hard. No paint lines. No bleachers.

Just a single ball and some boys standing around dribbling with more effort than rhythm.

I was less than impressed.

Then a voice cut through the air. "Line up!"

And that was the first time I heard Coach Peter Akindele.

Coach Akindele and the Warlords

Coach Akindele didn't have fancy clothes. He didn't wear a whistle or carry a clipboard. But he had a presence like a force of nature. Steady. Grounded. Confident.

He didn't wait for things to be perfect. He made things possible.

There were no shoes for us. No cones. Only one ball to go around. But Coach Akindele had vision. And from that dusty court, the Warlord Basketball Club was born.

We weren't tall or skilled. Most of us didn't know the difference between a travel and a dribble. But Coach Akindele looked at us like we were already a team. And so we became one.

The Warlords.

We didn't just play. We fought. We sweated. We grew.

We wanted to compete with the rich schools, the ones with polished courts, full jerseys, team buses. Schools like the Bells, Covenant University—anywhere where kids played for fun, not survival.

But they never came to us.

They said our court was unsafe. That we weren't ready.

So, we went to them.

We scraped together transport money, begging neighbors, skipping lunch, pooling spare coins. We walked long distances when we couldn't afford the *okada*[11] fare. Sometimes we arrived late to the game, sweaty, legs already shaking, with just five players and no substitutes. But we competed.

We lost often, but every point we scored felt like a declaration: *We belong here.*

And then—when I least expected it—*he* came.

Meeting Coach Peter Ahmedu

He stood on the sidelines, arms folded, eyes scanning the court like a scout. Coach Peter Ahmedu.

Tall. Calm. Magnetic.

---

11. A motorcycle taxi used to transport single passengers.

"That's the national team coach," my brother whispered.

I couldn't help but laugh. "Here? Why?"

But he wasn't just passing by. He was *watching*. And when practice ended, he made his approach.

"You," he said, pointing at me. "Have you played before?"

"No sir," I said. "I play soccer."

He smiled. "Then you already know how to move. Now shoot."

I took the ball, aimed at the bent rim, and flung it.

Clang.

Wide. Miss. The boys laughed.

Coach Peter didn't. "Again," he said, calm as ever.

So, I tried again. And missed again.

"Again."

His voice wasn't stern. It was inviting, like he could see something I didn't. Each miss started to feel less like failure and more like permission—to learn, to grow, to try.

After practice, he pulled me aside. "You've got something," he said. "Hustle. Grit. Raw talent. I can work with that."

Then he added, "Come to my house tomorrow. I want to show you something."

The Poster That Changed Everything

The next day, I walked to his house, nervous energy bouncing in my chest. It wasn't a mansion, just a modest home with a cement yard where the smell of training sweat hung in the air. Several boys were already there, dribbling, working, focused.

Then I saw it: a poster on the wall.

Three players. Bold, intense, mid-action. Gary Payton. Ray Allen. Olumide Oyedeji.

Coach Peter pointed to the third. "You know him?"

I shook my head.

"He's Nigerian. From here. He played in the NBA."

I froze. In an instant, my mind stretched beyond the compound walls, beyond Sango Ota.

"You mean…*here*?" I asked. "From this kind of life?"

Coach Peter nodded. "Exactly this kind. And he made it."

That poster cracked something open in me, like a match striking a sopping-wet rag and still catching fire.

That night, lying on the mat back home, as rats scrabbled in the corners and mosquitoes buzzed in my ears, I stared at the ceiling and whispered, "If he can do it…why not me?"

A New Love

That was it.

Basketball had claimed me.

It wasn't just a game anymore. It was a calling. *My* calling.

I woke up early to dribble before breakfast, even when there wasn't any. I spent hours perfecting the moves I saw on posters and scratched CDs. I trained without shoes or socks—just skin, sweat, and sheer power of will.

I didn't have jerseys. I didn't have a court that was truly safe. But I had something better: belief.

From Coach Akindele, I learned how to scrap and lead. From Coach Peter, I learned how to dream with structure, how to sculpt chaos into discipline.

I was no longer the boy hawking vegetables in the street. I was an athlete. A warrior. A scholar of the game.

The Court That Built Me

That broken court at School III? It turned out it wasn't broken at all. It was blessed.

It was where I learned how to fail and keep going. It was where I took my first shot. Where I met the men who saw in me more than I could see in myself. It was where survival started to look like something greater. Like purpose. Like destiny.

It was where I realized that I didn't have to stay where I was born. That I didn't have to be defined by hunger or rats or rusted dreams. That greatness was possible—even for someone like me. And it all began the day my brother dragged me to School III.

6

A New Kind of Court

You never forget your first real love—not the kind that breaks your heart, but the kind that builds it.

For me, it wasn't a person.

It was a broken basketball court.

Cracks, Rust, and Belief

The court at School III wasn't much to look at.

Cracked concrete, uneven ground, weeds sprouting from its edges like wild hair. The backboard was a warped piece of plywood nailed to a rusted iron pole, bent forward as if it were bowing under the weight of its years. The rim leaned slightly left, its orange paint faded and peeling, no net, no give. You had to bank the ball just right or pray for mercy.

There were no painted lines. No bleachers or scoreboard. Just boys with bare feet, worn dreams, and hearts that beat in sync with every dribble.

And yet, to us, it was everything.

That court was the only place we could truly breathe free. It was our cathedral. Our compass. Our refuge.

Our dusty patch of Sango Ota didn't belong in a Nike commercial. But for us—boys raised on red dirt and rationed hope—it was sacred ground.

The Fire Beneath Our Feet

We played barefoot until our soles toughened like old leather.

In the dry season, the sun turned the concrete into a conflagration. You could fry an egg on it. Every sprint scorched our toes, but we ran anyway.

In harmattan, the rain made the court slick and treacherous. We slipped, we fell, we bled, but we kept going. Our ankles turned red from the earth. Our heels blistered from the friction, our toenails blackened from impact. Sometimes they peeled clean off. We'd wrap our feet in strips of old cloth and keep playing.

The pain became part of the game. Every cut was a credential.

Every bruise was proof that we were becoming something the world hadn't yet noticed.

Basketball players.

Not because we had uniforms. But because we had purpose.

The Ball That Wouldn't Bounce

Real basketballs were rare, like rainfall in the dry season.

When we did get one, we treated it like treasure. But when it popped, which it always did, thanks to rocks and overuse, we didn't throw it away. We revived it.

We'd take the deflated ball, find a smaller rubber one—usually a cheap ball meant for street soccer—and stuff it inside the leather shell like a heart transplant. Then we'd walk it to a roadside vulcanizer, the local tire repairman.

He'd smile, pat the ball, and say, "Ah, you boys again?"

For a few naira, he'd patch it up like a *danfo* tire, using glue, rubber, maybe even a layer of inner tube.

The ball never bounced right afterward. It wobbled, drifted, spun oddly. But it bounced enough, and that was all we needed.

A real basketball cost more than a week's food. For families like ours, that wasn't an option. But patched-up balls kept our dreams alive.

Each crooked bounce was a heartbeat.

Each wobble was a whisper murmuring that we might still have a shot.

Car Tires for Soles

As for shoes, that was another story.

My first "basketball shoes" were someone's cast-off sneakers discovered near a dump site, one size too small, the soles barely hanging on, the stench permanent. I wore them until they disintegrated.

Then came the car tires.

We found an old one discarded by the road, sliced it open, and cut out two pieces roughly shaped like feet. We took them to a local cobbler, a gray-haired man with a hammer that looked older than me.

He stitched the rubber onto the bottoms of my busted shoes and layered glue until they held.

The result?

Heavy.

Awkward.

Ugly.

But indestructible.

And that was my version of the Nike Air.

We couldn't afford brands, but we had innovation. We ran without cushion. We jumped without spring. And we landed hard, every single time.

But we kept moving.

Because the court didn't care how you looked. It only cared how much you gave.

The Discipline of Dirt

Coach Akindele was the first man who taught me that basketball was more than a game.

When he showed up one day at School III—quiet, thin, eyes like flint—he didn't bring gear or sponsors. He brought standards.

If you were late, you ran.

If you complained, you ran more.

If you didn't respect the court, he sent you home. Coach Akindele didn't make exceptions for poverty.

He demanded excellence through effort, not privilege. He used tires for defensive drills.

Stones to mark cones. Old planks to teach footwork.

We practiced bounce passes with balls that didn't bounce, ran suicides under the sun until we saw stars, shot at a rim that leaned like it wanted to escape.

But we got better.

Repetition. Repetition. Repetition.

No excuses. No shortcuts. Just work.

Beyond basketball, he taught us character.

We learned to greet our elders, clean our space, speak with respect. We learned gratitude, humility, responsibility.

"I'm not building players," he told us. "I'm building men."

And we believed him.

The Court That Was Our Classroom

In a country with more than 13 million out-of-school children, we were lucky.

Our school wasn't a building. It was that broken court.

We learned math through spacing, physics through angles and arcs. Passes and pick-and-rolls taught us communication, and teamwork taught us leadership. Sweat honed our discipline.

Coach Peter was our professor, his whistle our syllabus. We didn't sit behind desks. We stood in huddles.

And we listened—not because we had to but because we wanted to *become*.

Something Sacred

Even now, when I walk into state-of-the-art gyms with polished floors and digital scoreboards, I carry that first court with me.

I see the stones we used to mark the three-point line. I hear the thump of bare feet on burning concrete. I feel the rough weight of a patched ball, smell the rubber soles cut from car tires.

Because that court, that forgotten slab of concrete in Sango Ota, built me.

Without fans or funding, it gave me something no money could buy.

Grit.

Hunger.

Purpose.

That court didn't whisper promises. It shouted truth. If you wanted something, you had to bleed for it.

It was the first place I truly believed that greatness was possible—all because Coach Peter looked at a barefoot boy and saw a future.

Because my teammates—shirtless, tired, fierce—played like warriors.

Because even without a net, even without shoes, we were seen here. This wasn't a place where we were just surviving. We were becoming.

Although I didn't grow up in privilege, I grew up in purpose. And it all started on a court where nothing was perfect, but everything was possible.

44 | A New Kind of Court

7

Coach Peter's House

A Man Who Chose Us

Coach Peter Ahmedu was more than a coach. He was a legend. He had already walked the path many of us could barely dream of.

Former head coach of Nigeria's National Women's Basketball Team. Technical director. The man who led the Dodan Warriors, one of Nigeria's most respected professional clubs.

He had stood courtside at AfroBasket. He had walked the floors of international arenas. In Nigerian basketball, his name echoed through history. And still he chose us.

Not the kids with polished shoes or wealthy families, nor the ones in gated schools or fancy training programs.

He chose the boys with patched balls and blistered feet. He turned stubborn dreams into chances to succeed. He chose the kids the world had already counted out.

And in doing so, he rewrote our futures.

A Home with Structure

Coach Peter's house wasn't large or grand, but it had something I hadn't felt in a long time.

Peace.

His home had order. Structure. Direction. His walls were decorated not with riches but with intention, proudly displaying tidy bookshelves, framed pictures of past players, a faded prayer calendar, a whistle resting on the table. It smelled like focus—sweat, soap, and roasted plantains from the vendor across the street.

Every time I stepped through his front door, something in me settled down.

Back home, I lived in chaos. My family's apartment was overcrowded, noisy, unstable. But in that small Lagos home, I found something deeper.

Hope.

Not the quiet, wishful kind but the kind that moves furniture, that makes room for you. The kind that looks you in the eye and says, "You belong here."

Lessons That Had Nothing to Do With the Game

Coach Peter taught much more than just basketball. He taught life itself.

Between drills and sprints, he'd ask the kind of questions that left us in silence.

"What kind of man do you want to be?" "What legacy are you building?" "Who are you when no one is watching?"

I froze the first time he asked me that last one.

Who was I, really?

I had spent so long just trying to survive—finding my next meal, dodging disappointment—that I had never stopped to ask what kind of person I was becoming.

But Coach Peter forced us to confront ourselves. To confront our futures.

And for many of us, it was the first time we had ever believed we were worth the reflection.

The Poster That Changed Its Meaning

One evening, I found myself staring, once again, at the NBA poster on Coach's wall. It was always there, silently watching us train.

Gary Payton. Ray Allen. Olumide Oyedeji.

The first time I saw it, it had lit a fire in me, and that was something I couldn't forget.

He made it. From Nigeria. Just like me.

But on this particular evening, something shifted.

I noticed something new, something beyond the jerseys and the spotlight.

Olumide had come back.

He'd built camps. Supported young players.

He didn't just make it. He brought others with him.

And that's when it clicked: *Success* wasn't the end goal. *Service* was.

Greatness, real greatness, doesn't hoard the light. It reflects it.

That night, I whispered to myself, "I don't just want to be great. I want to help others find their greatness, too."

My First Real Camp

The moment I heard about the Olumide Oyedeji Basketball Camp, my heart beat like a drum.

It was at the National Stadium in Surulere, Lagos—a dream location for kids like us.

The whispers claimed that scouts would be there. That someone could get discovered.

But dreams often come with a price. I lived in Sango Ota, Ogun State. Lagos wasn't exactly next door.

And I had no relatives there. No place to stay. No money.

I begged my friends for help. One kind soul gave me just enough to cover the application fee. I scraped together a few coins and submitted my form. The only thing I received in return was a T-shirt, the first new item of clothing I'd worn in years. It became my uniform, a symbol of belief—both mine and theirs.

Then came the problem of transportation.

I woke every morning at 4 a.m. and bused my way through the chaos, dodging hollering conductors, squeezing into *danfos* packed tighter than jerrycans of palm oil.

By 8 a.m., I'd be sweating on the court.

At lunch, others unwrapped jollof rice, beef, plantains, ice cream, all packed with love. I was given a pouch of Milo[12]—free, thanks to Nestlé.

---

12. A brand of vitamin-fortified chocolate milk that is particularly popular in Australia, South America, and some areas of Africa and Asia.

That Milo became my meal, my strength, my symbol of hunger and hope. Cup after cup, I drank it daily, filling my stomach with courage and calories.

After camp, I'd beg for a ride home. Sometimes I was pushed away. But other times, someone would reach out, pull me into the bus, and let me sit on their lap. No words. Just kindness.

That camp broke me. And then it built me.

It reminded me that this journey would be hard. But it also reminded me of how deeply I wanted it.

Shiloh: The Game That Made Me a Story

Then came the Shiloh basketball tournament at Winners Chapel.

Thousands had gathered from across Africa to worship. But amid the sermons and songs, there was also a tournament—fierce, competitive, and deeply spiritual.

I was selected to play.

We fought through every round, clawing our way up the bracket.

Then came the final.

That morning, I hadn't eaten, and not by choice. There was simply nothing left.

After the quarterfinal, I drank *garri*, letting it soak into my belly like a blessing.

By the last ten seconds of the final game, we were down three points.

An inbound pass darted my way. I ran off a screen to the corner, and the ball found me.

Two dribbles.

I rose.

The defender crashed into me.

"Foul!"

Three free throws.

The crowd screeched—some praying, others taunting.

I breathed.

First shot, *swish*. Second, clean.

Third?

In.

The crowd exploded.

I was hoisted into the air like a champion.

And for the first time in my life, I wasn't the underdog. I was the hero.

"Pastor, marry me!" people screamed. Even girls I'd never met joined the chant.

The name stuck.

And later that night at church, a man from the Dodan Warriors, Alexander Ujoh, approached me.

He smiled, pointed, and said, "Pastor, you're going places."

I've never forgotten that.

An Invitation That Changed Everything

Sometime after, Coach Peter pulled me aside again. "I'm moving to Lagos," he said.

My heart dropped.

But then, "I'm starting something new—a real academy. Warriors Basketball Academy. And I want you there."

I blinked. *Me?*

The barefoot kid with tire soles for shoes?

It felt impossible. But when life offers you a door, even if you don't know where it leads, you walk through it.

Joy in Every Dribble

We had no uniforms. No water bottles or highlight reels. But we had joy.

Laughter when someone slipped trying to dunk. Chants after a successful block. Celebrations after every game, win or lose.

Basketball was more than just a sport.

It was a culture. A family. An identity.

In every dribble murmured, *We matter.*

Through every pass, we told each other, *You're not alone.*

We didn't need approval. We had each other.

A Growing Dream

Coach Peter began to talk about scholarships, camps, scouts. At first, I just smiled politely, not really believing.

But then I saw it.

One kid got recruited. Then another. Suddenly, "impossible" lost its meaning.

Basketball wasn't just a game anymore.

It was a passport. A megaphone. A lifeline.

And every single dribble was one step closer to freedom.

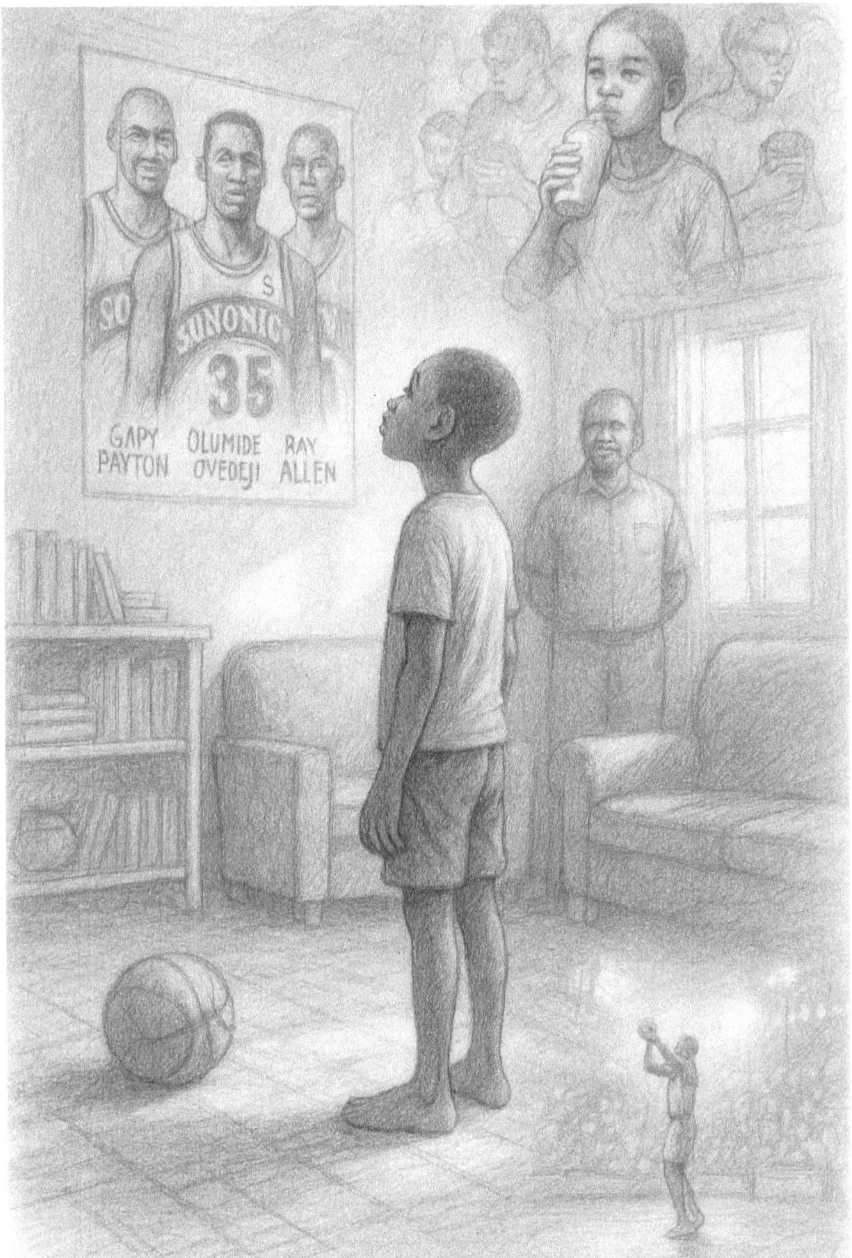
SONICS
35
GAPY PAYTON
OLUMIDE OVEDEJI
RAY ALLEN

II

Part Two

The Fall and the Fight

8

The American Dream Begins

Warriors Basketball Academy: Where Everything Shifted

When I joined Warriors Basketball Academy in Lagos, it felt like stepping out of one world and into another.

This wasn't Sango Ota anymore.

This was Lagos, the stage where boys became men and men chased glory, where street dreams met structure, where you either rose to prominence or disappeared.

Everything felt bigger, not just the city. The noise was deafening. The pressure was crushing. And the players…

The players were much bigger. Tall. Polished. Known.

Many had already been to elite camps. Some already had agents whispering promises. A few had even secured scholarship offers.

They walked with confidence. With clean sneakers and shoulders that didn't bow under the weight of hunger the way mine did.

There I was: 6'2", lanky, quiet, unknown. But in that environment, I felt short.

And not just in height.

In history.

My teammates included Charles Okwandu, a 7'2" center who would later play at UConn alongside Kemba Walker and win the 2011 NCAA National Championship.

There was Temidayo Adebayo, a 7-footer from Montrose Christian School, the same place where Kevin Durant had sharpened his gifts. Temidayo would go on to graduate from college in Philadelphia.

Dele Coker stood at 6'10" and eventually earned a scholarship to St. John's University in New York.

These weren't just players. They were pathways made flesh.

Others, like Solomon Alabi and Joseph "Katuka," walked those same cracked courts in Ilupeju and, eventually, through the shimmering halls of the NBA.

They were giants in every sense.

And I was a thin blade of grass fighting to grow, reaching for the light from the shadows of their greatness.

A Hunger Beyond Food

We all lived at the Warriors camp on Adeoya Close in Mushin. The compound was tight, humble—a cluster of hope stitched together with mismatched mattresses, shared buckets, and a rotating stove.

There was no luxury. No air conditioning. Just steel beds, concrete floors, and the sound of sneakers squawking through our late-night dribbling drills.

But what we lacked in comfort, we made up for in fire.

We shared not just a roof but pain, passion, and prayers. When one of us had an embassy appointment, the entire camp stopped. We ironed each other's shirts and polished our only shoes. We shared travel money and held each other close like soldiers before battle, waiting for their ticket out.

We would gather at the gate to watch our teammate climb into a car and head to the airport. We clapped and cheered even though our own hearts ached.

Some returned waving the coveted visa in the air. Others came back in silence, eyes red with rejection.

Some never tried again.

Some scraped and saved for another shot.

And every time, I whispered the same silent plea: "God, let my turn come, too."

According to the U.S. Department of State, Nigeria has one of the highest student visa rejection rates in Africa, often below 35%. The application process was a maze of form after form: I-20, DS-160, SEVIS, financial statements.

And the final decision came down to a single five-minute interview.

Many in Lagos applied, but the word on the street was that Abuja had better odds.

Fewer people. Less pressure. A chance.

And so I chose.

Betting Everything on Abuja

The journey from Lagos to Abuja is more than 470 miles. More than just a trip, it's a pilgrimage.

And I had no money.

But Coach Peter believed in me, again. He paid for everything: transport, food, hotel, fees. It wasn't just generosity. It was a declaration: *I believe in your future more than your present.*

He handed me the ticket with the same care that a father might give his son a sword before battle.

Waiting

The U.S. embassy in Abuja was a fortress.

Outside, hundreds of hopefuls waited, their eyes laden with dreams. Some clutched folders. Others clutched only faith.

I stood in line, palms sweaty, whispering the only prayer I knew could voice my fragile hope: "Let this be the day."

When my number was called, I stepped forward, my feet heavy as stones being pulled from the ground.

The officer barely looked at me. "What school are you going to?"

"The Rock School in Florida."

"Why that school?"

"Because it gives me a chance. To play, to study, to live a life I've only imagined."

He stared. No emotion. No response.

Then, in a motion so small it felt invisible—*stamp*.

"Hope to see you in the NCAA next year."

And that was it.

I walked out trembling, holding my passport as tenderly, carefully, watchfully as a newborn.

When the air outside hit me, so did the tears—not from sadness, but from the release of years of pressure, pain, and prayers, too many to count. I was going to America.

My First Flight

The day of my departure, I barely slept.

I had never seen an airport before. Never packed a bag. Never sat in a plane. Everything was noise and light and movement—all overwhelming for a boy from a ten-room compound.

The airport smelled like metal and jet fuel. My heart beat so loudly I thought the other passengers must be able to hear it.

When the plane lifted off, I looked out the window and saw Nigeria shrinking beneath me. The roofs. The roads. The red dirt. All fading into a blur as the ground dropped away below us.

I whispered again, "We made it, Mama. We made it."

Like Landing on Another Planet

Landing in America felt like stepping onto another planet— with no guide, no translator, no familiar air.

I pressed my forehead to the plane window as we descended, watching the strange, orderly grid of Florida's streets, the neat rows of homes, the glass buildings that shimmered under the sun like they belonged to another species of life.

I should have been excited. But inside, all I felt was a low, persistent panic.

I came from a one-room apartment in Sango Ota, a space where six people shared one mattress, where water had to be fetched by hand, and electricity came like a rumor.

Nothing in that life prepared me for what I was walking into.

Culture Shock

Florida greeted me like a wave crashing against the shore. It was loud. Bright. Strange.

Even though I spoke English, I didn't understand anything. The slang, the jokes, even the speed of the words were all unfamiliar. I nodded and smiled, trying to hide my confusion.

My new coach, Coach Svend, picked me up and drove me straight to Burger King. I had never even seen a hamburger before, let alone tried one.

I took one bite and gagged. The bread was cold. The meat tasted like rubber. I forced it down.

My host family was kind in the polite, American way. They smiled. They offered help. But beneath the smiles, there was a gap I couldn't name, only feel.

They didn't cook. The kitchen was filled with frozen meals and plastic-wrapped snacks. That first night, they served me a bowl of something white and mushy.

Grits.

I had never seen grits before. I scooped a spoonful, raised it to my lips, and immediately gagged.

The texture was gluey, the flavor dull. It felt like eating warm sand. I laughed quietly, a nervous laugh that quickly dissolved into guilt. *Don't be ungrateful*, I told myself. *This is your shot.*

Hunger would humble me. So I swallowed it, forcing down every bite.

The Shower and the Shame

Later that day, I went to the bathroom to take a shower. I stood there alone, staring at the knobs, trying to decode the system.

Back home, we used buckets. There were no faucets or knobs. No choice of hot or cold. The water was just either there or not.

I spent nearly an hour trying to figure it out.

I couldn't ask for help. I didn't want to feed into the stereotypes I feared they already believed—the ones from Tarzan movies and cartoons where Africans wore loincloths and ran through jungles. I could feel those false images pressing down on me like fog.

You cannot be that, I told myself. *You cannot confirm what they assume.*

Yearning

That night, I lay on a strange bed in a strange room, staring at a white ceiling. There was no mosquito net, no familiar breathing, no distant hum of a generator.

Just absolute silence.

I missed home. I missed my mother's laugh. I missed the chaos of the compound. The aroma of jollof rice dancing through narrow hallways. The rhythm of street life.

But I reminded myself, "You didn't come here for comfort. You came here to fight."

Wings

Joining Warriors Basketball Academy gave me a vision. Coach Peter gave me a path. That visa gave me permission. And that plane gave me wings.

But none of it came easy.

It came with hunger. It came with rejection. It came with cracked courts and patched shoes and prayers sighed into empty bowls.

And now?

Now every time I lace up my sneakers, every time I hear a ball echo in a quiet gym, every time I rise for a shot, I remember the boy who once drank Milo for lunch and ran barefoot on broken concrete. I carry him with me.

Because I didn't just come to America to play. I came to become.

9

Proving Myself

The Fight Begins

At The Rock School, the court was polished. The balls bounced true. The nets were new and unmended. There was no need for that here.

But the biggest battle wasn't on the court. It was inside me.

I had to learn to speak up. To ask for help. To find my place in a world that felt too big and too fast.

I trained hard. I listened more than I talked.

At night, I studied plays and practiced my shots when no one was watching.

Every day, I became less of the barefoot boy from Sango Ota and more of the young man who believed in his budding dream.

Questions That Cut

One day in class, a girl stared at me—not just a glance, but a long, awkward gaze.

Finally, I walked up and asked, "Is something wrong?"

She tilted her head and asked, eyes wide with genuine curiosity, "Do you wear clothes in Africa? Have you ever killed a lion or ridden one to school?"

I wanted to vanish.

But instead, I smiled.

"No," I said. "I've never seen a lion in my life. And yes, I wear clothes. Probably more than you do."

She laughed. I did, too. But inside, I crumbled. Because I realized something vital.

I wasn't just here to earn a scholarship. I was here to defend my dignity, to fight for my identity in a world that didn't understand it.

Eyes on Me

At The Rock School in Gainesville, the expectations came fast and loud.

I wasn't just a player. I was the player from Nigeria.

The one they brought all this way. And for that, they expected magic from me.

Every sprint, every drill, every pass, it felt like a spotlight was burning into my back.

I was jet-lagged. I hadn't slept in days. The food was foreign. My body hadn't adjusted. And yet, I was expected to compete.

I tried. God knows I tried. But my first scrimmage was a disaster. I was slow. Disoriented. I missed passes. Missed switches on defense. Got torched by players I could have locked down back home.

After the game, Coach pulled me aside. His words were simple but sharp: "You'd better get it together."

He didn't yell. He didn't curse.

But his tone pierced deeper than any scream.

The Pain Begins

Soon after, a sharp pain began stabbing my shins.

I chalked it up to overtraining. *This is what it means to go pro*, I told myself. But it only worsened.

At a summer tournament in Gainesville, I could barely run. Every step sent fire up my legs. My body had betrayed me.

I was benched. I sat in shame watching games I should have been playing.

That night, I cried in silence. No lights, no noise. Just me and the ceiling.

"Don't blow this," I told myself. "This is your only shot."

Every night, I iced my legs with frozen packs like a ritual. I took ibuprofen like vitamins. Anything to stay on the court.

Finally, one day, I approached my coach, fear hanging heavy in my throat.

"Coach," I asked, "what if no school wants me…because of my injury?"

He looked at me not as a burden but as a believer. He rested a gentle hand on my shoulder.

"The way you play?" he said. "There are definitely schools that will want you. Just keep pushing. I believe in you."

That was the first time in weeks that I didn't feel like a liability. That day, my belief came rushing back.

$200 and the Call

To survive, I worked small jobs—mowing fields, cleaning benches, doing whatever others didn't want to do.

Within three months, I had saved $200. It felt like treasure.

Then the call came.

My father was dying. Prostate cancer.

In Nigeria, diseases like this don't announce themselves. They don't knock. They invade.

Slowly, silently, they lay siege on your body.

There's no regular screening, no early diagnosis, no affordable treatment. More than 70% of Nigerians lack access to even basic healthcare.

My father was slipping away, and I wasn't there.

I didn't hesitate.

I wired my full $200 home through Western Union. Money meant for my food, my soap, my clothes.

But he needed it more.

The Fall

A few weeks later, I was called to the principal's office.

"You owe money," they said.

I explained everything. The transfer. My misunderstanding. That I thought the I-20 covered a full scholarship—like the paper said.

The principal just shrugged. "We say that to help speed up the visa process."

My stomach dropped.

Everything I had sacrificed, all the pain I had endured—none of it mattered.

Two days later, I was informed that my scholarship had been revoked. My flight back to Nigeria was already booked. Coach Svend came to the house to deliver the news.

I collapsed.

I didn't cry; I wept. I curled into myself on the cold floor. Every mile I had traveled undone. Every prayer unanswered. Every voice back home that had mocked my dream vindicated.

"You? Make it in America?"

"We told you."

Maybe they were right.

But God Wasn't Finished

That night, I fell to my knees.

I cried from a place so deep, it had no words. The kind of cry only God could understand.

"If this is what I must go through to save my father," I whispered, "then I accept it. But please…please don't let this be the end."

I had nothing left. No home.

No shoes. No court. No future.

But I had that prayer.

And God heard it.

Because even as everything around me was falling apart…He was writing a resurrection.

10

The Fall

The night before my scheduled flight back to Nigeria, I lay in a bed that had never really felt like mine.

The mattress creaked beneath me. The sheets smelled faintly of detergent and something older—something like endings. My suitcase sat zipped beside me, quiet and heavy, like a graveyard of dreams. Inside were the clothes Patrick, one of the international students, had given me when I first arrived in America. Folded with care, each one weighed more than fabric should.

A pair of jeans. A toothbrush.

The battered sneakers I once believed would carry me to college glory.

Each item whispered memories—tryouts, practices, prayers whispered beneath my breath in locker rooms. But tonight, they weren't trophies. They were tokens of shame, evidence of my failure. My return would not be triumphant. It was wrapped in silence and sorrow.

Outside, the rain came hard.

It lashed against the windows with the same fury I felt boiling in my chest. It was as if the sky itself was grieving with me, loud and unrelenting.

I didn't cry that night, but not because I was strong. I had simply run out of tears.

I couldn't call home. I couldn't bear to hear my father's voice. How do you explain the weight of a broken dream to the person who believed in it the most? I wasn't going home with a scholarship. I was going home empty-handed.

The Coldness of Departure

The airport didn't care who I was.

It buzzed with life as people rushed toward vacation plans, business meetings, reunions. They moved with confidence. Purpose. With money in their pockets and itineraries in their hands.

And me?

I stood in the corner, alone. There was no one to send me off.

No money. No plan. Just a return ticket to the very same streets I had begged God to rescue me from.

I didn't even have a dollar to make a phone call. So I did something I had never done before: I asked strangers.

"Excuse me, sir…Do you have a dollar so I can make a call?"

Some ignored me like I didn't exist. Some turned their heads with practiced indifference. Others said "Sorry" before I could even finish speaking.

Eventually, I managed to convince someone to let me make a few calls until I reached someone I had met briefly in Boston. I dialed his number with shaking hands and explained my situation, desperate for kindness.

His response hit like a slap: "You probably stole the money. That's why they're deporting you."

I stood there, stunned, with the phone pressed against my cheek, his words ringing in my ears like a cruel bell. Then I slowly hung up.

And in the middle of the terminal, surrounded by people moving forward in life, I sat down and broke.

Boston: The Unplanned Delay

My itinerary had five legs, each designed to send me farther away from the dream I had carried for years. Gainesville to Atlanta. Atlanta to New York. New York to Boston. Boston to Frankfurt. Then home.

But when I reached Boston, something changed.

When I arrived at the gate for my flight to Frankfurt, exhausted and hollow, the gate agent looked at my ticket, then at me, and frowned.

"This ticket isn't valid."

I blinked. "I'm sorry? What do you mean, 'it's not valid'?"

"I don't know, but you can't board this flight."

I tried to explain. I pulled out my passport, my crumpled papers. "Please," I said, my voice cracking, "I'm not running from anything. I'm going back to my country."

But rules were rules.

Security was called. I wasn't handcuffed, but I might as well have been. Shame clung to me like sweat, and people stared as I was escorted to the airline counter.

By the time we reached it, the final flight of the day had already left, so the airline rebooked me for the next day. They handed me a hotel voucher—a simple piece of paper that felt like a lifeline—and sent me on my way.

It was 10 p.m.

I hadn't eaten all day. I had no phone and no money, just my backpack heavy with sorrow and a delay that felt more like divine intervention than coincidence.

A Final Cry for Help

In that hotel room, I dropped to my knees. Pride had long since left me.

I didn't whisper or perform. I could only sob.

"God, if this is truly the end…please, let it have purpose. But if there's still a path for me, please show me."

Then, like a final flare into the dark, I opened Facebook.

I started messaging everyone I knew—classmates, old teammates, family friends. Some didn't reply. Some sent prayers but no help. Others assumed I had done something wrong.

But then a message lit up my screen.

Ejike Ugboaja: A Lifeline

Ejike Ugboaja. A name I knew well. The first Nigerian drafted into the NBA straight from Africa. A legend. I had never met him, but I had studied his journey like scripture. His story was proof that it could be done.

Desperation pushed me to write him.

Sir, I'm stranded in Boston. My scholarship was revoked. I have no place to go. Please help.

I stared at the screen, not expecting anything. Then...

Stay at the airport. I'll figure something out.

Within hours, Ejike got a hold of a man in Boston, Simon Akowe, another Nigerian brother I had never met but who agreed to pick me up.

He didn't ask for a resume or interrogate me about what had happened and why.

He just showed up.

The Mercy of Strangers

Simon greeted me at the airport with the kind of warmth that needs no translation. He didn't ask questions. He simply saw a boy drowning in disappointment and offered me dry ground. He took me into his home, fed me, gave me a place to sleep.

For the first time in days, I laid down and breathed. The room was small, and the bed was hard, but to me, it felt like a palace, like mercy.

The next morning, after I'd rested, Simon handed me a Greyhound bus ticket.

Destination: Atlanta.

A New Chapter

I arrived in Conyers, Georgia, with nothing but faith. Ejike welcomed me into his home.

Inside were other young Nigerians—each carrying their own story, their own wounds, their own wild hope.

We slept on mattresses pushed close together. We cooked simple meals and shared whatever we had. We were a family forged by a shared fire.

It wasn't comfort, but it was belonging. And it felt like a resurrection.

For the first time in weeks, I slept without fear—not because the storm had passed but because I had found shelter inside it.

This Was Not the End

The ticket said I was flying home to failure. But God had other plans.

That night in Boston wasn't the end of my dream but the threshold of something bigger, something I couldn't see then but would one day look back on and call grace.

11

The Door That Didn't Close

A Fragile Brotherhood

Atlanta was a fresh start, but it came wrapped in uncertainty. After all I had endured—the revoked scholarship, the night stranded in Boston, the miracle of Ejike's intervention—I arrived in Atlanta with nothing but hope and a backpack. Ejike Ugboaja, the man I once only knew through headlines and highlights, welcomed me like a little brother.

But Ejike's home wasn't just his and mine. It belonged to all of us, a patchwork family of young Nigerian athletes, each with a dream too stubborn to die. We came from different cities and backgrounds, but all our stories shared a common thread: We had nowhere else to go.

The living room floor became our mattress. The couch, a shared pillow. The kitchen? Often empty, except for hope.

But we shared stories in the dark. Laughed between waves of fear. Split slices of bread like communion.

There was no structure. No school. No guarantees.

Just a fragile brotherhood built with the bricks of survival.

Hunger Wears a Heavy Face

When Ejike left for Europe to continue his career, reality descended on us like a cold wind.

Before, we were scraping by. Now, there was nothing to even scrape with.

What little money he left behind disappeared fast. Some of the other boys had family who occasionally sent support. But not me.

Some days, we had one meal. Many days, none.

We rationed noodles like currency. Poured water into empty stomachs and called it dinner.

We joked through the pain. At least laughter was easier than surrender.

One night, I lay curled on the hardwood floor, my stomach knotting in waves. There was nothing left to eat. I prayed for food. I told God I didn't need a feast, just a crust of bread.

"God…just one more day. Let me make it one more day."

But hunger doesn't just settle in your belly. It gnaws at your confidence. It whispers doubt into your bones.

Fear That Knows No Rest

At night, fear invaded our house like smoke. Thin but constant. Suffocating.

Every time the doorbell rang, my pulse spiked. Every time a car slowed outside, my stomach flipped.

I wasn't enrolled in school. My visa status was unclear. I was a ghost in a system that didn't see me.

I stayed inside, off the radar, off the map. I didn't go out unless absolutely necessary. I tried not to call attention to myself. Even my breath felt too loud.

Every ring of my phone felt like an omen, every unknown number like a noose.

"God…I came this far. Please don't let it end here."

And then—on a day like any other, when we had almost nothing left—came a knock that changed everything.

The Knock of a Lifetime

He filled the doorway like a statue carved from Herculean strength—tall, composed, authoritative.

Coach Curtis Berry.

Former University of Missouri standout. Retired professional athlete.

High school coach in Atlanta.

But to me, he was a complete stranger.

"Are there any kids here looking for a school?" he asked.

We blinked, unsure if this was real. I stepped forward.

So did Robert, another Nigerian athlete who had been living with us.

Coach Berry's voice was firm and candid, but there was kindness behind it.

No empty words. No pity.

"I want to help. But not just because you can play. I want to help you become men."

No one had ever said that to me before.

The First Ride

The first thing he did was take us to eat. We hadn't had a hot meal in days.

As I sat before a plate of rice and meat, the aroma alone made my eyes water. But it wasn't the food that fed me most; it was his questions.

Not "What's your vertical?" or "How many points can you score?" but "What does your mother mean to you?" "What's your biggest fear?" "What kind of man do you want to become?"

I didn't know how to answer. I wasn't used to being seen for anything beyond my talent. But something inside me softened. For the first time in months, I felt safe.

He told us about Mount Vernon Presbyterian School, a private institution with rigorous academics, well-kept facilities, and the kind of structure I hadn't had since leaving Nigeria.

I didn't say much on that ride. I had learned to guard my hope. But in the quiet of that car, I felt a flicker I didn't want to quench.

Meeting Dr. Jackie

That night, Coach Berry introduced us to his wife, Dr. Jackie Walters.

Yes, *that* Dr. Jackie. The brilliant OB-GYN. The reality TV star. The powerhouse.

But at that moment, she wasn't a celebrity. She was Mama.

She greeted us with a warmth that felt like home. She served us rice, chicken, and vegetables—real food, seasoned with care. She asked about our health, our families, our hearts.

And when she hugged me, I nearly broke. Because in that embrace, I felt my mother's arms again.

That night, as I lay in a soft bed with clean sheets and a full stomach, I whispered "Thank you" to God over and over again.

The GISA Rule

But good things rarely come without hurdles.

According to the Georgia Independent School Association (GISA), student-athletes couldn't live with their coaches. If Robert and I were to attend Mount Vernon, we needed legal guardianship outside the Berry home.

Most people would have thrown up their hands. Coach Berry didn't even blink.

Before we knew it, they found a guardian.

They rented us a modest apartment.

They paid the deposits, filled out the paperwork, and never once asked for thanks.

They didn't just open a door. They carried us through it.

Back on Track

Mount Vernon accepted us. Just like that, I was back in school. Back on a team.

Back on a path I thought I had lost forever.

Coach Berry was unyielding. He demanded discipline. No shortcuts, no excuses.

We showed up early. We worked harder. We stood straighter.

And more than a coach, he was a mentor. He poured into us like we were his own.

Meanwhile, Dr. Jackie fed us, checked our grades, tracked our health. More importantly, she asked the question no one else had thought to: "How are you *really* doing?"

They didn't just keep us in school. They gave us a home.

A Promise to Pay It Forward

One night during an early team meeting, we sat on the hardwood floor, sweat still fresh on our brows, sneakers still laced.

Coach Berry stood at the front. "This is about more than basketball," he said. "This is about the kind of man you'll be when the ball stops bouncing."

And in that moment, I made a promise in my heart: *One day, I'll be the knock on someone else's door. One day, I'll carry a kid the way they carried me.*

I had come to America with nothing but a dream. I had almost lost it all.

But through the kindness of strangers who had made themselves family, I was no longer holding on by a thread.

I was holding onto purpose.

12

Dr. Jackie and a New Home

A Mattress Like a Miracle

After months of sleeping on hardwood floors, on worn-out couches, and in borrowed space, the apartment Coach Berry and Dr. Jackie arranged for us felt like something straight out of a dream.

It was nothing extravagant—not by American standards, anyway—just a two-bedroom space with faded carpet, creaky cabinets in a narrow kitchen, and walls so thin, you could hear your neighbor sneeze. The blinds didn't close all the way, and the bathroom door squeaked.

But to me, it was a palace.

There were beds. There was running water. There was light—and not just from the fixtures overhead but from the certainty that no one was going to take it away.

The first night I lay on that mattress, I didn't sleep.

I just stared at the ceiling—white, cracked in one corner, stained from some long-forgotten leak—and breathed.

Not the shallow, anxious breaths I had grown used to in survival mode, but slow, deep, grateful ones.

The silence wasn't the kind I had once feared—the silence of shame or fear.

This was a peaceful silence, like being wrapped in a warm whisper: *You're safe now.*

Even the soft hum of the refrigerator felt like music. That sound—consistent, steady, alive—reminded me we had more food than we needed today and, more importantly, a place to store it.

I slept like a child that night.

Because for the first time in a long time, I could.

A World I'd Never Seen: Mount Vernon

Stepping into Mount Vernon Presbyterian School was like walking onto a movie set. Everything gleamed, from the polished floors to the lockers that swung smoothly and silently on their hinges. The classrooms smelled like books and clean air, not the schoolrooms overcrowded with chalk dust and sweat that I'd grown up in.

The students had perfect teeth, perfect backpacks, and perfectly timed laughter. They had the kind of confidence that can only come from never knowing hunger, never missing tuition fees, never going to bed afraid.

They had summer homes.

They had ski stories from Aspen.

They talked about brands I couldn't pronounce and places I'd only seen in glossy magazines.

And I walked in with a duffel bag and shoes scuffed by struggle.

My accent clung to me like a second skin. I wasn't just different; I was alien. In the cafeteria, I sat quietly. I studied how they talked, how they moved. I felt invisible some days. Other days, I felt like I was on stage, eyes watching my every move.

But I reminded myself, I didn't come here to fit in. I came here to rise.

More Than a Coach and a Doctor

Coach Berry wasn't just a coach.

He was our French teacher, our driver, our mentor, our disciplinarian. And for all intents and purposes, he was our father figure.

Every morning, like clockwork, he honked his horn outside our apartment, signaling that it was time for school.

We'd race down, half-awake, backpacks half-zipped, and pile into his car.

He'd drive us to school, drop us off, and remind us to keep our heads up.

After class and practice, he'd do it all again—reversing the route and making sure we got home safely. Some nights, we'd ride in silence. Other times, he'd use the ride as a lecture hall: "You've got to think long-term." "Nobody owes you anything." "Excuses don't live in this car."

And then there was Dr. Jackie.

She wasn't a reality star yet. But to us, she already shone brighter than the cameras could ever capture.

She was an OB-GYN with a full schedule, delivering babies, running her clinic, yet somehow she always still found time for us. She kept our health in check. She packed care bags. She made sure we always had clean clothes and enough to eat.

Most of all, she was something I hadn't known since leaving Nigeria: the comforting presence of a mother.

Warm. Gentle. Loving. They weren't just providing food or furniture. They were building a foundation for our future, and consistency, compassion, and care were their rock-solid bricks.

Life Lessons That Don't Come From a Classroom

Living in that apartment came with its own curriculum—the kind of learning they don't test you on but that life grades you by.

We had to split grocery money, sometimes calculating it down to the last cent.

We learned to cook rice without burning the bottom, eggs without breaking the yolk.

We learned to clean, not just because it was expected but because we finally had something worth keeping clean.

If the power went out, we lit candles and kept going. If we were late for school, we didn't make excuses. As Coach Berry had taught us, "You're not a victim. You're a warrior."

We took ownership and learned, hardship by hardship, how to be men.

Finding My Rhythm Again

At Mount Vernon, something inside me began to shift.

I wasn't the smartest in the classroom, but I studied harder than most.

I wasn't the flashiest on the court, but I hustled like it was life or death.

The pain still echoed in my shins, a reminder of the battles I had already fought, but I pushed through.

Because I had something stronger than pain: purpose.

Coach Berry noticed. Dr. Jackie nurtured it. And slowly, I began to believe it, too.

Every time I stepped on the court, I remembered the barefoot boy back in Sango Ota—chasing dreams on cracked concrete, dribbling with a patched-up ball, wearing shoes cobbled together from car tires and prayer.

That boy was still alive in me. But now he had a roof.

He had mentors.

He had a second chance.

The Birth of New Dreams

In the quiet of that tiny apartment, with our mismatched dishes and loud refrigerator, something sacred was taking root.

We were no longer just surviving. We were becoming.

Becoming students.

Becoming athletes.

Becoming men.

We were learning that grace and growth don't require luxury—just love and structure.

And I began to dream again.

Not wild, unreachable dreams but purposeful ones. Rooted in gratitude.

Watered by resilience. Unshakeable.

Unstoppable.

III

Part Three

Purpose From Pain

13

The Setback No One Saw

By the time I reached my junior year, pain had become more than an inconvenience. It became my shadow.

It moved when I moved. It lurked behind every sprint. Sank its teeth into every jump. Resurrected doubts with every step.

It wasn't the kind of soreness you shake off after a tough practice. This was different. Sharper. Deeper. Like something splintered was burrowing into my shins. It gnawed at the bone whenever I pivoted or cut to the basket.

After practice, I sat on cold bathroom floors clinging to ice bags shrouded in towels, pretending they were enough. I popped ibuprofen like candy. I didn't expect to feel better—that was out of reach—I just wanted to feel normal.

But I never told anyone how bad it truly was. In my mind, pain was the price of greatness. Pain meant I was earning something, moving forward.

I believed that if I could just keep going, something would break through—something besides my body.

The Warning Signs

One evening after practice, I limped over to Coach Berry and asked in a low voice, "What if I can't get a scholarship because my pain is slowing me down?"

He studied me for a moment, then nodded slowly. "You've got heart, Adeola. There are plenty of NAIA schools that would be lucky to have you. Don't stop. Just keep giving everything."

His words were gentle but powerful, the kind that stay with you long after they're spoken. I held onto them like a lifeline.

But my body had other plans.

Playing Through It

By senior year, I couldn't fake it anymore. My legs refused to lie for me.

Each sprint felt like dragging weights through fire. My defense slowed. My first step, once explosive, lost its spark. The joy I once felt on the court was being consumed by dread.

Scouts noticed. Coaches passed me up. The calls stopped coming.

It was supposed to be my year—the one where I could cash in, where the barefoot boy from Sango Ota would finally taste the harvest of all his hard labor.

But instead, I found myself just sitting on the sidelines, watching others get their offers, smiling through gritted teeth and fractured dreams. Inside, I was crumbling.

I had crossed oceans, battled poverty, narrowly avoided deportation. And now I was losing to my own bones.

The Silent Class

Somewhere in the mess of my schedule, I got placed in an art enrichment class.

It wasn't strategic or even intentional, just a gap filler. I sat in the back—quiet, tired, mostly going through the motions.

One day, I picked up a pencil and began to sketch a few shapes, lines, a smattering of shadows. Scribbles from a place too deep for words.

The teacher stood behind me for a long time, but I was so absorbed in my task that I didn't notice until he spoke.

"You've got something," he said.

I looked up, confused.

"Have you ever thought about using this to get into college?"

I almost laughed.

College? Through art?

Basketball was supposed to be the plan. Art was just an escape. A breath of fresh air when the weight was too much to bear.

But the next day, he came back with canvases, paint, and brushes and laid them on my desk.

"Just create," he insisted.

And so I did.

Painting the Pain

Each stroke of the brush became its own kind of therapy, a way of speaking without words.

I painted barefoot boys dribbling rubber balls, their eyes lit with longing.

I painted mothers stirring empty pots, trying to make something from nothing.

I painted fathers standing at windows, watching their sons disappear into dreams they couldn't follow.

I painted my story.

And my teacher saw it.

Without telling me, he submitted my work to the Savannah College of Art and Design (SCAD).

A few weeks later, he pulled me aside, beaming. "They want you," he told me. "They're offering a partial scholarship."

It wasn't everything. But it was hope.

And after months of running on fumes, hope felt like oxygen.

Another Blow

But life has a way of testing us right when we're on the verge of a breakthrough.

At the same time art was opening a door, my relationship with Coach Berry began to fray.

Too much pressure. Too many miscommunications. Two people trying to perform and survive and make sense of it all—clashing and colliding.

We argued. We misunderstood. And just like that, I was without a team, without a home, and without direction.

Again.

The Kindness of Strangers

That's when Mark Heiser, the school's athletic director, quietly stepped in.

He was the kind of man who didn't need to be loud to make a difference.

He and his wife, Kelly, offered me a place to stay.

No questions. No judgment. Just a warm bed and a safe space. It was Kelly's mother who first mentioned the College of the Ozarks—a small, tuition-free, work-study college in Branson. A small, tuition-free, work-study college in Branson.

Her voice held the kind of spark that made me believe it was worth a try.

So, I applied.

I had hope, but I reserved my expectations.

A Crack in the Door

A few weeks later, I received a call from Coach Steve Shepherd.

"I've heard your story," he said. "And I see your heart. We'd love to have you at the College of the Ozarks."

The words I had been waiting years to hear: *Yes.*

I'd have to sit out one semester, but I didn't care. I was going to college. I was going to rebuild.

I was going to start again.

14

Surgery and Survival

One Last Chance

When I arrived at College of the Ozarks, it felt like grace had cracked open a door no one else could see.

A tuition-free education. A new basketball team. A different state. A fresh beginning.

It was everything I had prayed for in those quiet moments alone with my dreams that refused to die, even amid fading chances.

From the outside, I looked like a kid who had finally found his footing.

But behind the polite smiles, behind the hustle on the court, behind the grateful posture, I was sheltering a secret.

And that secret screamed every time I walked across campus.

A Pain No Tape Could Silence

It wasn't soreness. It wasn't fatigue.

This was a pain that had buried itself in my bones—sharp, jagged, unrelenting.

I had carried it for years, from the dusty roads of Sango Ota to the bright gyms of Mount Vernon to the uncertain court of Gainesville.

I had trained my body to ignore it. Taught my brain to push through it. Convinced myself that pain was the inevitable toll of greatness.

But now the bill was past due.

Each sprint became a negotiation with gravity. Each game felt like walking barefoot over glass. Some mornings, I could barely heave myself out of bed. Some nights, I crawled to the bathroom.

But I stayed quiet.

Because when you come from where I come from, you don't complain. You survive.

You tape it.

You ice it.

You pray it away.

And you smile like it's all just a part of the plan.

A Door Swings Open

Then came Paul and Jen Elmore, an American couple with a reputation for generosity, especially with Haitian children.

They had heard part of my story, heard about my pain and my refusal to give up.

Maybe it was my eyes. Maybe it was the limp. Maybe it was God.

But they saw something in me, and they didn't avert their gaze or turn away.

Instead, they introduced me to Dr. Tally, a local physician.

Calm, kind, and thorough, he was quick to order X-rays.

When the results came back, he didn't speak at first, just studied the images with quiet disbelief.

Then he turned and broke the news: "Both of your fibulas are fractured. And based on the healing patterns, they've been broken for a long time."

I blinked. Had I misheard?

"Your legs shouldn't even be supporting your weight," he added, almost to himself.

I had been playing on two broken legs.

I wasn't being brave.

I wasn't being tough.

I was being shattered in silence.

Broken, But Not Beaten

According to the World Health Organization, nearly 60% of Nigerians pay for healthcare out-of-pocket. Less than 5% have access to proper orthopedic care or sports medicine.

For families like mine, an injury wasn't something you healed. It was something you ignored.

And so I had done precisely what I was taught to do: endure.

I had run on broken legs. Fought with broken confidence. Dreamed against broken odds.

But I never stopped moving. Because broken is not the same as beaten.

My body was bruised. My path was messy. But my spirit? Unshaken.

And somewhere beneath the fractures, the pain, the false starts, and the rejections, there was still one unbreakable thing left in me: faith.

My story wasn't over. It was just shifting.

And so was I.

The Knife and the Night

The surgery was scheduled at Skaggs Regional Medical Center, now CoxHealth, in Springfield, Missouri.

Both legs. One operation.

That night before the procedure, I lay in a small hospital bed, IV tubes in my arms, monitors quietly humming. The room smelled like antiseptic and cold steel. My heart was steady, but my mind raced.

I whispered prayers into the ceiling.

"God… I've survived poverty, hunger, abandonment… Please don't let me die here. Not on a hospital bed far from home."

I called my parents.

I didn't tell them everything, just that I loved them. That I was okay. That I'd call again soon.

Drowning on the Inside

The surgery went well—until it didn't.

The next morning, I woke up gasping for air. My chest was on fire. My lungs felt soaked. My throat burned like acid. The beeping around me sped up. Nurses rushed in.

I was drowning from the inside: I had aspirated. During the operation, fluid had entered my lungs. Suddenly, I was choking on life itself.

Dr. Tally came in, grave-faced.

"We may need to operate again," he said, almost apologetically. "But… there's a risk you won't make it." And then, "You should call your father."

At just twenty years old, thousands of miles from home, I was told to prepare for death.

But I didn't cry. I didn't panic. I prayed.

Lord, if this is how it ends, let it not be wasted. Let it mean something.

Then I looked up at the doctor and said quietly, "Do what you need to do. My life is in God's hands."

"I'll Be Back"

Before they wheeled me away, I saw them.

Coach Steve Shepherd, standing tall but shaken.

The assistant coach, silent, worried.

My teammate, tears in his eyes but nodding, holding on to belief.

A few administrators, clipboards in hand, eyes wide.

And in that moment, through all the tubes and beeping, I smiled.

"No worries," I reassured them. "I'll be back."

The Miracle

I closed my eyes, floating between worlds.

And then I opened them.

Dr. Tally stood above me, his expression unreadable. Finally, he shook his head slowly and said, "You made it. I don't know how, but you did."

But I knew how.

God wasn't finished with me.

The Silent Struggles We Carry

Lying there in that hospital bed, surrounded by machines and miracles, I wasn't just an injured athlete.

I was a symbol.

An emblem of the thousands of international students who suppress hidden pains in pursuit of American dreams.

In 2009, more than 671,000 international students studied in the U.S. We came seeking opportunity and carried with us wounds no one saw.

In Nigeria, more than 72% of health expenses are paid out of pocket. Most people, including my father, simply fight disease in silence. Prostate cancer took him not because it was untreatable but because it went undiagnosed for too long.

Where you're born can determine whether you live.

And so, I arrived in America both a dream and damage. With trauma. With injuries. With history.

And I was far from the only one.

More Than Legs

That surgery wasn't just about fixing my bones. It was about unearthing what I had buried.

It was about a body that had labored too long under the burdens of hunger, fear, shame, silence—and finally said *enough*. It was about stopping. Listening. Healing. Grieving.

It was about the truth I had never been allowed to voice: that pain unspoken is still pain. That wounds ignored don't disappear; they grow teeth.

But there, in that sterile hospital room, amid murmuring monitors and stark-white sheets, I came face to face with a new truth. My story was never just about playing basketball. It was always about finding purpose.

Why It All Mattered

I didn't survive just to chase trophies. I survived to build tables. To create lanes. To walk beside the next boy limping silently through life and tell him, "You're not broken; you're being rebuilt."

That surgery became my turning point. The pain could no longer be hidden. And neither could the calling.

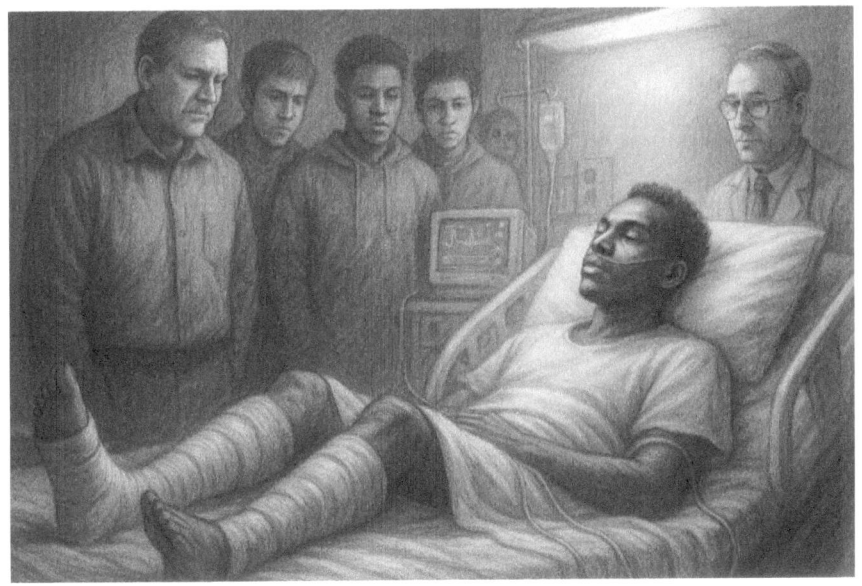

15

From Pain to Purpose: The AOA Foundation

Where Purpose Begins

Every sleepless night. Every rejection. Every cold floor, rolled-up mat, and silent scream from a fractured leg…

Every "no," every loss, every door slammed shut in my face…

They weren't just setbacks. They were seeds.

Seeds planted in the soil of suffering, watered by tears, and rooted in grit.

For years, I thought I was just surviving.

But in that hospital bed, lungs heavy, legs bandaged, future uncertain, I finally understood: Survival wasn't the finish line. It was the foundation.

And from that cracked concrete beneath my feet, something noble was beginning to rise.

To The Ones Still Waiting

As I slowly recovered from surgery—first with crutches, then a cane, then cautious steps—I began to feel something stir in me that was more powerful than fear: conviction.

I hadn't survived all this just to move forward. I had survived to reach back.

To the barefoot boys still dribbling patched-up balls under a relentless Nigerian sun.

To the girls walking miles to fetch water before school, skipping breakfast and still showing up.

To the students sitting in broken classrooms, too tired to dream but still hoping anyway.

I had been every one of them.

And now it was time to build for them.

The Birth of AOA

I didn't have money. I didn't have land. But I had a vision.

I launched the Adeola Ajayi Foundation (AOA) not from abundance but from a deep, defiant belief that my scars could build bridges.

It started as a whisper. *What if we ran a basketball camp? What if we fixed one court? What if we gave these kids what I never had?*

I shared my story.

I asked for help.

I said one thing to anyone who would listen: "Help me give back to the place that made me."

And people responded.

Because purpose is magnetic.

And pain, when shared truthfully, can become power.

Humble Beginnings, Unshakable Impact

The first AOA Basketball Camp was raw. A few donated basketballs. Hand-printed jerseys. Volunteers who brought heart instead of hype.

But it was enough.

Because when you gather kids in a dusty lot, hand them a ball, and say, "I see you," something shifts.

They stand taller.

They run harder.

They remember their names, not just the labels they've been branded with.

And from that first camp, a movement began to take shape.

What We've Done So Far

To date, the AOA Foundation has hosted five basketball camps in Nigeria, served more than 750 youth, reconstructed and maintained the only full basketball court in Sango Ota, and renovated an abandoned classroom into a thriving center for learning and mentorship.

Through our work, we have also donated more than 3,750 meals, 1,767 pairs of shoes, 1,437 jerseys and shirts, 900 pairs of socks, 300 toothbrushes and tubes of toothpaste, 595 tote bags, and more than 150 basketballs.

But this was never just about promoting basketball. This was about restoring dignity. About giving kids permission to dream bigger than their circumstances.

AOA Camp 2025: A New Standard

In 2025, everything changed.

We welcomed more than 200 campers, inviting them to not just shoot hoops but also experience a life-changing week rooted in dignity, community, and transformation.

Every camper received a backpack with hygiene essentials, six bottles of clean drinking water daily, and life skills workshops led by my mother, Dr. Jackie Walters, to help teach them leadership, cleanliness, identity, and purpose. They also received educational scholarships and top-quality sports gear.

We built a first aid and health station because in our community, even basic care was a luxury.

Beyond the court, we delivered twenty-five kegs of cooking oil and more than 1,550 pounds of rice to widows and struggling families in our neighborhood.

This wasn't charity. It was community restoration, empowerment in action.

The Unveiling of Noble Court

Then came the moment that shook me to my core: the launch of Noble Court. Not just concrete and paint, not just an athletic facility, but a monument to hope. A resurrection site. A living memorial to my late father, Idowu Ajayi, "ID Noble."

We built a full outdoor basketball court, painted boldly in black, orange, and white; seating for 200 spectators; two bathrooms with showers; a learning hall with classrooms, an office, a kitchen, a first aid room, and five restrooms; and murals with wave designs, African symbols, and quotes etched in walls and pavement.

And at the heart of it all, written loud and clear, was the message our children needed, the one I wished I'd had: *You may come from nothing, but you are not nothing.*

Legacies Immortalized in Names

We named the classroom building the Dr. Jackie Learning Hall in honor of my mother, the woman whose strength had kept me above water through every storm.

We named the seating area the Curtis Berry Champion Seating Stance for the man who gave me shelter, structure, and the gift of discipline.

These weren't just dedications but thank-yous carved in stone.

Legacy isn't what you leave behind. It's what you build into others.

Purpose Over Pain

There's a photo I keep close.

Me, standing in the center of Noble Court, hands on my hips, chin up, looking out not just at the horizon but at every invisible version of myself that got me here.

The me who played barefoot in the dirt. The me who sold vegetables on the street. The me they tried to deport. The one who slept hungry. The one that ran on broken legs and gasped for breath after surgery.

Despite it all, I'm still standing.

Because every scar became a sentence in a grander story, and every failure became a flame that refused to go out.

From Concrete to a Crown

Today, AOA isn't just a foundation. It's a movement.

A declaration that poverty doesn't erase potential. That cracked concrete can still grow kings. That barefoot dreams can still lace up and rise.

Because amid the dirt of despair, a seed was planted. And what bloomed? Something noble. Unshakable. Unstoppable.

Purpose.

16

Where My Feet Now Stand

Sometimes I sit alone in the early hours before the world begins its rush, savoring a lukewarm cup of coffee and the faint echo of birdsong beyond the window.

It's still quiet then, just enough to hear my own thoughts. The stillness feels sacred, like the earth itself is pausing to reflect.

In those moments, I find myself thinking not about the man I am today but the boy I used to be.

I can still see him clearly: a skinny boy with knobby knees and a stubborn spirit running barefoot down the cracked streets of Lagos. Dodging puddles and broken bottles with a sort of reckless grace.

The soles of his feet were worn thin, calloused like a second skin, but he ran like he was chasing something bigger than himself.

And maybe he was.

That boy squinted through dust clouds as they kicked up behind passing *okadas* and rickety yellow buses, chasing after a ball made from plastic bags held together with string.

He went to bed hungry so many nights, watching the ceiling above him blur with the kind of dizziness that comes from having an empty stomach and a full heart.

Still, every night, he whispered prayers into that cracked ceiling like it was the ear of God.

He tightened his frayed shoelaces like armor. He didn't have much, but he had faith.

The kind of faith that can't be taught.

The kind you cling to when everything around you is pushing you to let go.

He had nothing, yet he carried everything.

No basketball shoes, but he had a vision. No lunch, but he had a purpose. No place to truly belong, but he had the unshakable belief that, one day, he would build one.

That boy had every reason to quit, every excuse the world would've accepted. But he didn't.

He kept running.

What Basketball Gave Me

To the outside world, basketball is just a game. But to me, it was a lifeline. A language. A compass.

It didn't just give me a scholarship. It gave me a way to breathe.

Basketball became my soul's translator. When I didn't have the words to say, "I'm hurting," I showed up and played through the pain.

When I didn't know how to ask for help, I practiced until the lights went off.

When life felt too heavy, basketball held me up and whispered, *Keep going.*

It gave me more than access. It gave me a sense of belonging.

It brought me into rooms I could have never imagined entering otherwise. It connected me to brothers and mentors, to love and purpose. It gave me bruises, literal and metaphorical.

Surgeries that stitched up both my muscles and my masculinity.

It gave me heartbreak—the kind that bends you but never breaks you.

But most of all, it gave me perspective. Basketball taught me what most books can't: how to lead *through* pain, not around it. How to believe when the scoreboard is screaming that victory is impossible. How to rise when you've hit the floor so hard, your soul rattles.

What People Gave Me

Let me be clear: I am not a self-made man. I am God-made.

Community-made.

Love-made.

There were moments when I was one step away from collapsing. But grace met me every time, picked me up and dusted me off—always disguised as people.

My father, Idowu Ajayi, ID Noble, a man who set aside his own dream of being an artist so I could chase mine. He taught me that sacrifice is not weakness; it's legacy in motion.

My mother, my warrior, who fasted so we could eat, who wept in private but smiled in public, who laid hands on my chest when I was sick and whispered healing into my bones.

Coach Peter Ahmedu, the man who saw me on a broken court with no shoes and said, "You're a player." I didn't even believe it then. But he did.

Ejike Ugboaja, who could have ignored my desperate Facebook message but chose to answer. He saw a kid clinging to hope and extended his hand.

Simon Akowe, who welcomed me into his Boston home like I was born from his blood.

Coach Curtis Berry, who looked me in the eye and said, "Come in." And with those two words, I entered a life I never imagined.

Dr. Jackie, who wrapped me in her warmth, said, "I choose you," and suddenly, I had a mother again.

Mark and Amy Heiser, who opened their door as well as their hearts.

Mr. Kunath, who handed me brushes, peered into my pain, and told me it was beautiful.

So many names. So many hands. So many moments that stitched my soul back together.

And every step I take now is because someone carried me when I couldn't walk.

What Noble Court Stands For

Noble Court isn't just pavement. It's resurrection. A court built not from concrete but from memory.

Every inch is laced with pain repurposed into pride.

We painted it orange, black, and white. We lined the walls with quotes that outlast struggle. We painted murals of warriors and children and ancestors.

And we embedded Noble Court right at the heart of it all—named for my father, built for generations.

Dr. Jackie Learning Hall stands to the side, a classroom named for the woman who taught me that wisdom is love in action.

The Curtis Berry Champion Seating Stance lines the bleachers, a reminder that belief is sometimes the greatest gift of all.

And in the middle of it all are the faces of the next generation. Little boys with no shoes but big dreams. Girls with braids in their hair and fire in their eyes. Teenagers who carry invisible wounds but still show up.

And to every single one of them, I say with my whole heart, "You matter. You belong. And you are more than the circumstances you come from."

What Legacy Means Now

The day my son Isaiah was born, the world stood still.

He arrived at just 26 weeks—so small that I could cradle his entire body in one hand. Less than two pounds, surrounded and supported by a forest of tubes and wires.

I stood there in the NICU, trembling not from fear but from love.

When I gently placed my hand on his head, he smiled a tiny, flickering smile.

Through the chaos, through the machines, through the prayers, I saw light.

I saw my father in him. I saw myself.

That moment taught me something I'll never forget: that resilience is inherited. Fire runs through blood.

And legacy is not just what we leave behind but what we pass forward.

Where My Feet Now Stand

I now stand on American soil, but my roots grip Nigerian earth like a sacred tree that remembers every storm.

I speak on stages once closed to me.

I lead a nonprofit.

I raise sons who walk with my fire. I help others build brighter futures.

But I will never forget the boy with dust in his eyes and dreams in his chest.

He walks beside me still. And every morning, I ask him, "What footprints are we leaving today?"

Because legacy isn't about the shoes you wear. It's about the story each step tells.

To You, the Reader

Maybe you didn't run barefoot down the streets of Lagos. Maybe you've never slept shoulder-to-shoulder with five siblings on a thin mat. Maybe you don't know what it's like to pray over an empty pot.

But you know pain. You've carried questions. You've felt invisible. You've wondered if you were enough.

So I ask you now: What will you build from the things that tried to break you? What will you grow from the dirt that once buried you? What court will you raise, not for applause but for purpose?

Because no matter how cracked your concrete is, you were made for more.

So, rise.

Rebuild.

And leave footprints that matter.

17

Bonus Chapter: A Letter to My Father, ID Noble

The hardest words to write are the ones that ache before they even hit the page.

For years, I kept this letter tucked inside my heart, half-written in the silences after dreams, drafted in the pauses between prayers.

Not because I didn't know what to say but because I wasn't sure if I could survive saying it.

But today, I speak.

Dear Daddy,

There are moments when I swear you're still here walking beside me, your footsteps heavy but gentle, your voice low and steady like the wind before rain.

You didn't leave behind treasure maps or bank accounts. What you gave us was worth far more. You gave us your name, a name you wore like a crown even when life tried to bend your back beneath the burden of poverty.

I still remember the rhythm of your walk, the shuffle of worn slippers on cracked cement, the occasional cough you never complained about, the way you carried your silence like a suit of armor. You weren't loud. But your presence filled a room. You didn't have much to give in material things, but you gave us stories, wisdom, patience, and honor. That was your wealth. We inherited it in hunger, and now I pass it on in abundance.

Do you remember that day, Daddy? The one when the landlord banged on the door, and Mama sat on the bed, holding her breath? I was just a boy then, but I saw your shoulders square up like a man preparing for war. You stepped outside, spoke with dignity—never raising your voice, never begging—and somehow left that conversation with our dignity still intact. That was you. Quiet strength. Unshakable grace.

You told me once, "Adeola, don't chase titles. Chase impact. A good name will carry you farther than gold." I didn't understand it then. But I do now.

And Daddy, your name—Noble—isn't just remembered; it's engraved in stone.

Noble Court.

A full outdoor court in the heart of Sango Ota. Black, orange, and white. African patterns in bold strokes. We named it for you not just because people called you ID Noble but because you truly lived that word. You embodied it. You were nobility without a throne, a king without a crown, leading a family through famine with your head held high.

You couldn't afford to buy me sneakers, but your belief in me was better than Nike.

And now, Daddy, every time I step onto that court, I feel your spirit in the echo of bouncing basketballs, in the laughter of children, in the way coaches shout encouragement like fathers shaping futures.

You never saw me dunk. You never saw me graduate. You didn't live to witness the foundation bearing your bloodline's name or the camps that feed hundreds of hungry boys who remind me of us.

But maybe, just maybe, you already knew.

Maybe when you watched me tie my ragged laces or walk to the farm barefoot, you saw a glimpse of this future.

Maybe when you sold another painting for pennies just to buy us rice, you knew those colors would one day return, bold and bright, on a court in your name.

Maybe you always believed your struggle had a purpose, even if you never saw its full harvest.

I want you to know, Daddy, I remember everything. Every fast you suffered without complaint. Every time you sat in the dark so we could have a bit of kerosene for the lantern. Every prayer you muttered in Yoruba when you thought we were asleep. I remember how you'd sit beside me, brush your fingers over my shoulders, and murmur, "Strong boy. You're a strong boy, Adeola."

And I became one. Because you were my first mirror.

The world knows me now by many titles. Founder. Speaker. Coach. Author. Leader. But none matter more than this one: your son.

You are the reason I give, the reason I serve. The reason I return every year to Nigeria with shoes, meals, books, and dreams wrapped in duffel bags.

You are the heartbeat of this mission. You are the inspiration behind every scholarship, behind every "I see you" whispered to a child no one else believes in.

Now they call me Noble. But the truth is, I'm just echoing your legacy.

And when Isaiah was born at 26 weeks, so fragile, so tiny, wires cradling his breath, I saw you again. I saw your fire in him. When he smiled through the beeping machines, I knew he had inherited your resilience, the same resilience you gave me. Because our family doesn't give up. Our legacy doesn't give in. We rise, no matter how small our beginnings.

And I see you in him. Sometimes I can't help but wonder, *Is he your return?*

I'll never know. But I do know this: Your legacy is alive. Through him. Through me. Through every child whose feet now dance on Noble Court.

This is more than a letter.

It's a thank-you carved in memory. A monument in ink. It's me saying I didn't forget.

And I never will.

Rest well, ID Noble.

You were, and will always be, my first hero.

With all that I am,
Your son,
Adeola

18

Bonus Chapter: Dr. Jackie, My Mother, My Miracle

Some people know her from television—gliding across screens with poise and precision, her voice confident, her wardrobe flawless, her presence commanding.

They know her as "Dr. Jackie." But I call her something else: Mom.

Not just the woman who raised me but the one who formed me. Molded me. Prayed over me. Carried me through childhood and then through life.

To the world, she is a healer of bodies. To me, she is a builder of souls.

To many, she is a two-time cancer survivor. To me, she is a two-time champion of impossible odds.

To millions, she is a voice in medicine. To me, she is the quiet whisper that still echoes in my heart on the hardest days: "Adeola, you were made for more."

More Than Medicine

Growing up, I watched her more than she knew. I was a boy raised in the gravity of her example.

I saw her come home from long hospital shifts, shoulders slumped with exhaustion, feet swollen from standing too long in heels. But her smile was always there—for us. Even when her strength was gone, her love remained.

I saw the white coat. I saw the awards. I saw the patients who clung to her like she was oxygen. But what shaped me most weren't her titles. It was the way she lived when no one else was looking.

The way she knelt beside my bed and prayed.

The way she packed our lunches even when she had surgeries scheduled at sunrise.

The way she told me, tears in her eyes, "Adeola, God has a plan for you," even when the lights were off and the rent was late.

It was the countless times she said, "Don't stop. You're worth the fight," even when I felt like I wasn't.

She taught me that purpose has a pulse, and if you listen closely enough, you can feel it in the quiet acts of service, not just the loud victories.

The Hall That Bears Her Name

When it came time to build something lasting for the youth of Nigeria, there was no debate. No boardroom vote or hunt for the right name. I already knew.

It had to be hers.

The Dr. Jackie Learning Hall stands like a lighthouse in the heart of Sango Ota. Four strong walls built from concrete and care. It doesn't just house lessons. It preserves a legacy.

Inside, children sit on benches and learn math, reading, and all the life lessons my mother taught me. That dignity is not about what you own but what you give. That you don't have to be wealthy to make a difference: You just have to be willing.

The Hall reflects her resilience. Her faith.

Her ability to be everywhere at once and still be fully present in the lives of the people who need her most.

Moments That Matter

I will never forget the moment my mother walked into Noble Court for the first time.

She stood still at the gate, her eyes wide, her hand covering her mouth. The bright orange and black lines of the court stretched before her. Children were running around, playing, giggling. Music was blaring.

And then her eyes landed on the Hall.

Her name. Her work. Her heart. All etched into a building thousands of miles from where she began.

She cried. I cried.

In that moment, we weren't just mother and son. We were two seeds planted in different soils but finally blooming in the same garden.

Two generations, one mission: to serve, uplift, and heal.

My Forever Example

She is elegance with iron in her spine. A woman of science and of prayer. She walks into rooms with quiet authority and leaves them better than she found them.

When I lost my scholarship, when I slept on floors, when I thought my dream was dead, she reminded me that my calling hadn't changed—just the path.

When I had surgery on both legs, her call was a lifeline. She prayed over the phone like her words alone could knit my bones back together.

And somehow, they did.

Because when your mother is Dr. Jackie, even her prayers wear lab coats.

The First Home I Ever Knew

Before the sneakers. Before the courts. Before the foundation, the fans, and the flights, there was a woman who held me close and whispered into the ears of a hungry boy, "You are not a mistake. You are called. You are mine."

That was my first home. And no matter how far I fly, it still holds me.

Thank You, Mom.

You are the quiet behind my courage. The strength in my spine. The faith beneath my foundation.

There would be no *Footprints on Concrete* without your fingerprints on my soul.

You didn't just raise a boy. You raised a servant.

A giver.

A believer.

And I pray every day that my life—this work, this story—is a thank-you written in motion.

I love you with everything I have.

Forever your son,
Adeola

19

Bonus Chapter: Coach Curtis Berry, My Father, My Foundation

To the world, he's Coach Berry.

A towering presence. A respected coach. A former professional basketball player. A frontrunner in real estate. A pillar in every room he walks into.

But to me?

To me, he's Dad.

Not by biology but by something even more enduring: love, sacrifice, and example.

The Man Behind the Name

I didn't grow up with Coach Berry teaching me how to tie my shoes or reading me bedtime stories. I met him at a crossroads in my life, when my world was splintering and I was desperately trying to hold the pieces together with calloused hands and silent prayers.

He didn't enter my life with fireworks. He came like a steady breeze—quiet, consistent, powerful.

At a moment when I was hungry for belonging, he opened the door and said, "Come in."

And it was in that gesture, simple but sacred, that he became more than a coach. He became my father.

A Different Kind of Champion

Coach Berry has a résumé that could span arenas: professional basketball, real estate ventures, championship teams. But none of those titles carry the weight of what he's achieved in the hearts of the young men he's mentored.

He didn't just coach games: He coached character. He didn't just identify talent: He invested in futures.

He taught me how to own my mistakes, not hide from them. How to lead without crushing others. How to walk into a room with my head high—not because I had all the answers but because I knew who I was. "Your name is your first trophy," he told me once. "Protect it."

He taught me that manhood isn't in muscles or medals. It's in the way you stand, the way you serve, the way you stay.

The Sideline That Shaped Me

When it came time to design Noble Court, we knew there had to be a place for him. It couldn't just be in my heart. It had to be the heart of the space itself.

That's why we named the court's sideline seating the Curtis Berry Champion Seating Stance.

Beyond a row of benches, it's a monument to all the times he stood courtside, arms folded, eyes focused on both plays and potential. To all the moments he corrected me without shaming me and challenged me without crushing me. To every kid who needed someone in their corner and found him standing there.

Because every champion needs someone in the stands. And for me, for so many of us, he was always there.

A Father Worth Watching

Coach Berry never made it about himself. He never asked for recognition. But his impact is written in the lives of everyone he's coached, every home he's built, every lesson he's lived.

I watched how he treated my mother, Dr. Jackie, with tenderness and reverence. How he balanced strength with sensitivity. How he led quietly but never passively.

He was the steadying hand I needed when I was falling apart. He was the calming breath when I was caught in chaos.

When I faltered, he never used my failure as a weapon. Instead, he stood with me, firm but gracious. Teaching. Guiding. Staying.

Even when he didn't fully understand the wild dreams embedded in my heart, he didn't try to clip my wings. He just nodded and said, "Go get it."

That kind of fatherhood, rooted in freedom and grounded in presence, is rare. And I know what a gift it is.

Thank You, Dad

Thank you for showing up when you didn't have to.

Thank you for choosing me—not out of duty but out of love. Thank you for never asking me to be perfect, only honest, faithful, whole. You didn't raise a boy. You raised a servant.

A leader.

A man.

And now, as I step into my own role as a father, a mentor, and a builder, I carry your lessons with every step.

Because of you, I know what fatherhood looks like: steady hands, listening ears, a backbone of faith, and a heart wide enough to hold the weight of other peoples' dreams.

Reflection: Legacy in the Stands

The Curtis Berry Champion Seating Stance is more than a name painted on concrete.

It's a symbol.

Of a man who gave without spotlight. Who led without applause.

Who fathered without condition.

Every child who sits there sits in the shadow of greatness, not because of a trophy shelf but because of a man who never let go of a single kid entrusted to him.

Dad, I love you, and I honor you. Forever.

Your son,
Adeola

20

Bonus Chapter: A Letter to My Younger Self

Dear Adeola,

You don't know it yet, but you're walking on sacred ground. I know it doesn't feel that way—not in that tiny, suffocating 9x9 room where your ribs press against your siblings as you sleep, where your dreams fight for air between the cracked ceiling and the concrete floor. I know that to you, the world feels far away, like there's a glass wall between you and everything you wish for.

But I'm here to tell you that space isn't a prison. It's a womb. It's building you.

That hunger in your belly? It's more than emptiness. It's a seed. And what it grows into will one day feed thousands.

You are not cursed.

You are being carved.

I See You

I see you curled in the corner at night, your head resting against a bag of rice that's more hope than food. I see the way you stare at the ceiling, whispering to a God you're not always sure is listening. I see the way you pretend you're not hungry so your little brothers can eat. The way you hawk produce in the sun until your legs wobble. The way you dribble that ball barefoot on a cracked court, pretending that the echo of each bounce is the thunderous applause of a crowd that doesn't exist—yet.

You wonder if you're crazy.

Crazy to dream of America when you've never even seen an airport.

Crazy to believe your sketches could mean anything to anyone.

Crazy to think a boy from a face-me-I-face-you compound could ever matter in this big world.

Let me tell you something, Adeola.

You are not crazy. You are called.

What Feels Like Struggle Is Training

Every scar is sacred.

Every barefoot game, every skipped meal, every silent cry into your pillow—they're not signs of weakness. They're weights. And you, my boy, are getting stronger with every rep.

You'll carry that cracked court with you. You'll remember the sting of shame when kids asked why your uniform was so dirty. You'll remember the slap of hot pavement against your bare soles. You'll remember how it felt to be unseen.

And because of that, you will see others.

Because you know what it means to be without, you will build something that gives.

Because you know what it feels like to be voiceless, you will amplify others' voices.

So don't despise this struggle.

It's chiseling you into a man who will stand with kings and sit with orphans, who will raise courts and raise sons, who will heal where others have only hurt.

What's Ahead

You'll board your first plane with nothing but a secondhand suitcase and unshakeable faith.

You'll step into cold American nights, speaking a kind of English that makes people stare, holding back tears when their questions sting your dignity.

You'll sleep on floors. You'll go hungry, again.

You'll be told to go back to where you came from. You'll almost be deported.

You'll play on broken legs.

You'll pray you're not dying in a Missouri hospital after surgery.

But you'll rise.

You'll meet people, angels in disguise, who open their doors and call you "son."

You'll meet coaches, mentors, families who will recognize what your hunger has forged you into.

You'll walk onto stages. You'll teach. You'll build.

You'll return to that same cracked street. And this time, you'll be the one cutting the ribbon to a court painted with your father's name.

And little boys who once played like you will now play *because* of you.

Carry the Name

Your father's name, Noble, isn't just a word. It's a weight. It's a responsibility. It's a gift.

And you'll carry it with pride. With tears. With fire.

You'll carry your mother's faith in your bones. You'll remember how she whispered blessings over you while stirring rice with tired arms. You'll remember how she looked at you like you were already someone.

You are. You *always* were.

And one day, you'll look into your own son's eyes—eyes that are miniature versions of your own—and say to him what I'm saying to you now: "You were born for more."

Until then, hold on.

Even when the light goes out. Even when your shoes fall apart. Even when your friends leave.

Even when your stomach turns from hunger and your eyes blur from tears.

Hold on.

Because you're not just surviving this season. You're storing power.

Gathering wisdom.

Planting seeds that will outlive you.

And one day, when the world calls your name, you'll answer not just for yourself but for the entire village that raised you. For the boys still dribbling on cracked concrete. For the mothers still fasting so their sons can eat.

You are becoming a bridge.

So, don't stop now.

I'm waiting for you on the other side.

With love,
Your future self,
Adeola

21

Bonus Chapter: What the Concrete Taught Me

Legacy isn't built in one big, shining moment. It's built quietly. In the spaces no one sees. In the early-morning choices. In the late-night sacrifices. In the promises you keep even when you're tired. In the people you show up for when there's nothing left to give but your presence.

I used to think legacy was made of trophies, titles, and applause.

Now I know the truth: Legacy is carved in the things that really endure. In hearts softened by service. In lives transformed by love. In hands lifted. In stories told.

What the Concrete Taught Me

The court—both the cracked one I grew up on and the one I now stand on—became my classroom.

Not just in how to pivot or shoot but in how to live.

That concrete whispered lessons I now carry in my bones. But they're lessons for more than just athletes. They're lessons for anyone still trying to find their way in a world that forgets the quiet fighters.

Pain Is a Teacher, Not a Trap

Pain once wrapped itself around my legs like a chain.

Hunger. Rejection. The humiliation of trudging barefoot while others wore Jordans.

I used to think the pain meant I was cursed. That it was my prison. Something to be endured, not learned from.

Now I know it was carving me.

Pain shows you who you are when the noise dies down. It hones your faith. It nurtures your endurance.

If you listen, pain can become your professor. Let it teach you, but never let it cage you.

Dreams Don't Need Permission

Nobody gave me a pass. No scout handed me an invitation. No uncle in high places opened a door.

But I dreamed anyway.

I dared to believe that a boy with callused feet and borrowed clothes could one day fly across oceans.

Sometimes, you have to knock on doors.

Other times, you have to build the door from the scrap wood no one else wants.

Dreams don't wait for validation. Dreams don't knock. They kick.

Poverty Is Not Your Identity

I was born in lack, but I was not born lesser.

I used to apologize for where I came from. I tried to hide the holes in my clothes and my story. But since then, I've learned that poverty is a circumstance, not a definition. It may shape you, but it doesn't name you.

Speak to yourself in the language of kings.

Even if your world looks like rubble, remind yourself daily: *I am more.*

Character Over Clout

This world worships image. Likes. Followers. Shiny filters.

But character? That's all that remains when the lights go out.

Coach Berry once told me, "Who you are when no one is watching—that's who you really are."

I've learned to choose respect over attention. To keep my word, even when it's inconvenient. To honor the people who helped me get here, even if the world never sees them.

Flash fades. Character endures.

Greatness Grows in Community

I didn't rise alone. I was carried.

By my mother's prayers.

By my father's silent sacrifices.

By coaches who believed.

By strangers who opened doors.

You don't need to be the loudest in the room. But be the one who lifts everyone around you.

Be the one who shares their meal, their wisdom, their strength.

When you rise, bring others with you.

Give What You Never Had

I didn't grow up with mentors or proper shoes. I didn't grow up with consistent meals or clean courts.

So that's what I gave. Mentorship. Meals. Shoes. Courts.

Sometimes your greatest gift to the world is the same thing you once longed for the most.

Become what you needed. Because that's how chains break.

Faith Is the Foundation

When I had nothing else, I had God.

When I lost scholarships, when I was almost deported, when I lay in a hospital bed thinking it was the end, faith held me.

Not religion.
Not ritual.
Faith.
A whisper in the dark: *Keep going.*
Faith grounded me when success could have swelled my pride.
Faith reminded me that my story wasn't about me: It was about leaving a legacy of service.
Legacy is built daily, not in one grand act but in a ripple of small decisions.
It's in forgiving when it's hard, in showing up when no one claps. It's in saying yes when you're scared and loving people even when you're tired. Every time you choose humility over ego, Service over spotlight, integrity over impulse, you're laying bricks in your legacy.

Final Thought: Footprints That Don't Fade

Concrete is cold. Unforgiving. Hard.
But if you walk on it long enough, if you keep moving with purpose, you'll leave prints that outlast storms, silence, and time.
I don't want to be remembered for how high I climbed. I want to be remembered for how many people I reached during my ascent.
Legacy is not the crown you wear. It's the torch you pass.
So, whatever you're building, make it outlive you. Make it bless someone else. Make it holy.
Because success celebrates you, but legacy serves them.
And that never fades.

Poetic Outro

Build with tears, if that's all you have. Dream barefoot, if shoes aren't near. Walk the cracked ground with quiet courage, and leave behind footprints the world can follow.

22

Images

THE JOURNEY

The dreamers' feet

AOA Basketball Camp 2019

AOA Basketball Camp 2021

AOA Basketball Camp 2022

AOA Basketball Camp 2022

AOA Basketball Camp 2023

AOA Basketball Camp 2023

AOA Basketball Camp 2024

AOA Basketball Camp 2024

*From left to right: Dr. Damon Kimes, Addy Kryger,
Dr. Heavenly Kimes, Dr. Jackie Walters, Coach Curtis Berry*

Campers drinking Milo beverages during AOA Basketball Camp 2024

Milo Rep serving drinks at AOA Basketball Camp 2024

AOA Basketball Camp 2025

COMMUNITY IMPACT

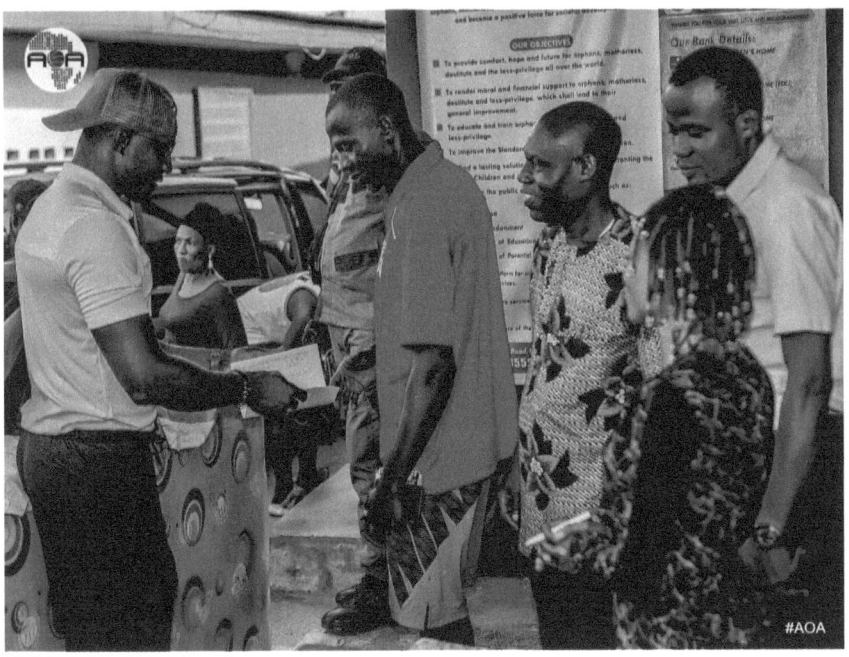

NOBLE COURT

Appendix: The AOA Foundation's Impact

AOA Foundation – Total Impact to Date

From a barefoot dreamer in Sango Ota to a global foundation changing lives, the Adeola Ajayi Foundation (AOA) has become a force of hope, purpose, and empowerment for children and families across Nigeria.

Through basketball, education, mentorship, and humanitarian relief, we've delivered tangible, lasting change:

Children Reached

- Impacted 950+ campers across six youth development camps
- Provided access to coaching, nutrition, leadership training, and safe spaces for growth

Facilities Built and Maintained

- Fully reconstructed and annually maintain Noble Court, Sango Ota's only outdoor basketball court
- Renovated a once-abandoned classroom to expand our educational space
- Opened the Dr. Jackie Learning Hall and the Curtis Berry Champion Seating Stance

Essentials Donated

- 3,750+ meals served
- 1,767+ pairs of shoes
- 1,437+ jerseys and t-shirts
- 900+ pairs of socks
- 300+ toothbrushes and tubes of toothpaste
- 595+ tote bags
- 150+ basketballs
- Clean drinking water daily during all camps

Education and Wellness

- 300 hygiene backpacks distributed (202 to campers, ninety-eight to community youth)
- Scholarships and sports equipment are awarded to top-performing children
- First Aid & Health Station launched to serve every camper's safety needs
- Life skills workshops covering leadership, hygiene, teamwork, and personal development led by Dr. Jackie Walters from *Married to Medicine*

Community Relief

- 4,650+ pounds of rice
- 75 kegs of cooking oil
- All these cooking supplies were donated to widows and low-income families in Ogun State

Noble Court

Noble Court stands as a tribute to Adeola's late father, Idowu "ID Noble" Ajayi. It was built not just for the love of the game but also to promote growth, healing, and legacy building. It features:

- 200-person seating capacity

- Two full bathrooms with showers
- A dedicated learning hall, office, kitchen, and first aid room, each with fully functional plumbing
- A mural wall with inspirational quotes and a wave design
- Curtis Berry Champion Seating Section to honor Coach Curtis's impact

Our Mission

AOA exists to remind every child, whether they belong to the concrete courts of Africa or anywhere else across the world: ***Your beginning doesn't define your becoming.***

This is what happens when pain is transformed into purpose and dreams rise from the ground up.

And we're just getting started.

To learn more, volunteer, or support our mission, please visit www.aoaimpact.com.

Call to Action

Leave Your Own Footprints

If this story moved you—if you saw pieces of your own struggles, your own strength, or your own hope in these pages—then let it move you to action.

This book is not just a memoir. It's a movement.

It's a call to rise, to give, and to build—***for their futures***.

Behind every cracked court in Nigeria, behind every hungry child with a dream too big for their village, is a story waiting to be rewritten.

And you can give them the pen.

Here's how you can leave your own footprint:

- **Donate to the AOA Foundation:** Your support funds life-changing basketball camps, builds safe courts, delivers meals, and gives underprivileged youth the tools they need to dream.
- **Share this story:** Tell your friends. Post about it. Use your platform! Every share is a spark that lights the way *for their futures*.
- **Sponsor a dreamer:** Whether it's sneakers, school fees, or a bowl of rice, your gift can change the entire direction of a child's life.
- **Invite me to speak:** Bring this message to your school, your company, or your church.

Let's inspire hearts, spark conversations, and build bridges between worlds.

Stay Connected

Website: www.aoaimpact.com

Instagram: @aoafoundation

Facebook: AOA Foundation

Email: ad@aoaimpact.com

Final Remarks

From cracked concrete, something noble can rise. Help us build courts of hope. Help us feed futures. Help us prove that where you come from doesn't define where you're going. This is not just my story.

This is *For Their Futures.*

#LeaveFootprints
#AOACares
#FromTheGroundUp
#ForTheirFutures

About the Author

Adeola Ajayi is a Nigerian American speaker, nonprofit founder, community builder, and former athlete whose journey from the slums of Lagos to the stages and courts of America has inspired thousands around the world.

Born into extreme poverty and raised in a 9x9 room with five siblings, Adeola grew up playing basketball barefoot on cracked concrete and dreaming of a future far beyond the limitations of his surroundings. Against all odds—and through faith, mentors, and relentless resilience—he earned a basketball scholarship that brought him to the United States.

After enduring injury, heartbreak, and homelessness, Adeola turned his pain into a new purpose by founding the Adeola Ajayi Foundation (AOA Foundation), a movement dedicated to transforming lives through sports, education, and service. He is the visionary behind Noble Court, a world-class hub of basketball and mentorship in Sango Ota, Nigeria, named in honor of his father.

Today, Adeola lives in Kansas City, where he continues to bridge cultures, communities, and generations. As the proud father of Elijah and Isaiah, he remains committed to leaving lasting footprints both on and off the concrete.

You can connect with him on:

🌐 aoaimpact.com

f facebook.com/aoafoundation